THE THEORY OF
TREEVOLUTION

CHRISTOPHER
STAGG

❧❧✦↯✦❧❧

❧❧✦↯✦❧❧

Paperback Edition: August 21, 2025

ISBN: 9 780975 165713

Editor: Katie Lowe

Cover design/layout: Matt Pike

❧❧✦↯✦❧❧

CONTENTS

For my remarkable children

Alex and Lauren

and our amazing grandsons

Zander, Rory, Maverick and Zane.

May you always be able to experience the joy of nature

AUTHOR'S NOTE

Writing a work that challenges the current thinking and belief systems of animal and human origins from a totally different perspective to the status quo is not perhaps the wisest thing for one man to do. Particularly a man who has no relevant academic qualifications to give credence to his writing. However, I do have an inquiring mind, a sometimes-annoying penchant for asking too many questions, an off-beat sense of humour, the benefit or otherwise of taking time to think things over and hopefully, a reasonably mature perspective on life that generally can only be gained from over 75 years of experience.

It has taken over 36 years of thought and research to bring this theory to light. Irrespective of the many, easily verifiable facts presented, I certainly do not expect everyone to agree with the concept of this work. All I ask of anyone who reads on, is for them to keep an open mind, and ultimately, an open heart, so they can see the potential benefits Treevolution has to offer humankind, the prime reason for it being written.

INTRODUCTION

I have always believed that our strong connection to trees is far deeper than just the draw to their visual and practical aspects. I have felt this ever since I was a small boy. One day, I begged my parents to let me replant a shrubby tree they were digging out of the back yard because it was dead. I just knew it wasn't, and I wanted to save it. Fortunately, they agreed to let me transport it to a small area around the side of the house near my bedroom window, on the proviso that I did the lifting, hauling and replanting on my own, which I duly did. The joy of seeing that tree budding with leaf less than a year later has never left me.

Perhaps it was this memory that subconsciously guided me to a remarkable discovery about our far deeper connectivity with trees than most would think possible. What I have uncovered sheds new light on many key aspects of our everyday lives – religion, medicine, science, our health, and even the forces that dictate our working lives and choice of lifelong partners. The strangest thing is, the discovery was so obvious and has been in front of us for so long, it has literally been a case of not seeing the wood for the trees.

As I was reading one day, my mind steered me to wondering about the formation of the English language. Who decided on 26 letters for the alphabet? Who decided what letters would be accorded to each word used to define objects, feelings, plants, animals and everything else? Why is the word 'dog', 'God' spelled backwards? Is there a deeper meaning or is it just mere coincidence? Why is a beekeeper called an apiarist, a word surely more suited to someone who makes a living trying to mimic celebrities, or more logically, an anthropologist who studies primates?

Was there some ordained group of people long ago who chose something to be named, then selected a number of letters for the purpose, drawing them at random out of a bag as if playing a game of Scrabble, and using them to form a word? I wondered if our language had evolved randomly, organically or according to some pattern or guiding process. Suddenly, an image came into my mind, and the link between humanity and trees just seemed to jump off the pages at me.

In a way, this flash of insight was like those 'magic eye' pictures, where you stare at an image of a seemingly meaningless pattern of dots and colours in a certain way and suddenly, a three-dimensional image appears. Many people never get to see what the hidden image is, simply because they are looking at it the wrong way. I couldn't believe it at first, but when I began to research words and knew what I was looking for, I came to realize the English language contains countless inferences to the role of trees being involved in its development – and that they have been desperately trying to communicate with us.

I assure you, my state of mind as I reached this conclusion was not influenced by the ingestion of mind-altering substances or liquids containing alcohol. As you read on and begin to discover more about the remarkable life of trees, you will begin to understand how they communicate with each other, to the point where the possibility of them also being able to interact with us does not seem unreasonable. The message the trees appear to be conveying is that humans are heading down a path that could lead to their and our destruction. I formed this view based on the timing of significant changes in human endeavour over a period in history that coincided with the development of the words and language I surmise indicates they have been trying to communicate with us.

THE THEORY OF TREEVOLUTION

fter humans first evolved, they, along with most other animals, coexisted well enough with trees, at least until a few hundred years or so ago. For millennia, humans used trees to create fire, tools, weapons, building materials and so on, but not in a way that adversely impacted the vast forests of the world. However, with the arrival of the industrial revolution in Britain in the 18th century, this peaceful coexistence began to change dramatically.

With mass production came the need for raw resources on an unprecedented scale. The products generated in this new industrialisation created more demand for building materials than ever before. These were needed to construct factories, housing for workers and their families, and the ships needed to freight goods to the four corners of the world. Populations throughout England and then much of Europe grew to match demand for manpower to run the air polluting, coal-fuelled factories. More land was cleared for the agriculture required to feed the growing masses. History records the effects of various plagues and epidemics on human populations, many brought on by diseases that thrived in the packed cities supporting this rapid and unprecedented move away from a more natural and sustainable way of living. The wise trees of the forests in Britain sensed the damaging future impacts on human wellbeing – as well as their own – and through communication means that we are yet to understand, they have been trying to alert us to take action for our own mutual good.

This is all well and very noble if what I have deduced is correct. I can certainly see why the trees would be aggravated if their own numbers were being reduced. One thing that puzzled me was the implication in their messages that they seemed to be more concerned for human welfare than their own. To my way of thinking, if I was a tree and word came around that human populations were going into overdrive and chopping us down like there was no tomorrow, any message I'd send would be along the lines of bugger off, or as a tree rooted in soil might say, sod off! After more research, which I will elaborate on throughout the rest of this work, the answer became clear.

Trees care for humanity because we are their descendants.

My theory is this. Human and primate descendancy, along with that of many other creatures, especially mammals, can be traced back to species of intelligent trees. The differences in evolutionary outcomes is affected by the intelligence and evolutionary progress of the tree genus from which each species originated. The trees passed on their knowledge to their mobile tree offspring via a means of communication we may someday come to discover and understand – a language that contains a constant reference to trees.

If the statement above gives you cause to shake your head and roll your eyes in disbelief, consider for a moment a slight spelling adjustment to the words in the following paragraph to make them read as they sound.

Every nation is referred to as a *countree* (literally a count-of-trees). Within each *countree*, we live in houses, placed in rows called S-*tree*-ts. To locate someone's address we use (at least until more recent times when satellite navigation systems became prevalent) a *directree* (which directs us to a specific tree).

The odds of the use of the word 'tree' in this logical manner being coincidental would be infinitesimally small. Over the course of history, words change in spelling and meaning. New ones are constantly added, and others fade from everyday use. However, the fact so many important and commonly used words in the current English language contain a reference in spelling, pronunciation and direct relationship to trees in their meaning provides an undeniable guidepost to our origins.

With this in mind, I have assumed any English words ending in –tary, –tery, –tory and –try, all pronounced 'tree', have come about through the ability of our ancestral trees to influence their human offspring in the formation and meaning of many words in the English language. The most obvious example of this influence on connecting the spelling of a word, its pronunciation and its meaning with our tree ancestors is *forestree* (forestry), literally meaning 'the science and practice of planting and taking care of trees.' For the rest of this work, I have spelled all words as I believe our tree ancestors intended them to be. For example: hereditary becomes *hereditree*, country becomes *countree*, ancestry becomes *ancestree* and so on.

The following is an example to show just how significant and logical the theory of treevolution is.

In any *countree*, an *elementree laboratree* study of the *biochemistree* of our *respiratree* and *circulatree* systems enables us to trace our *hereditree* traits back through *histree* to link our *ancestree* to a single *solitree* species of tree!

The odds against this direct reference to the word 'tree' being in so many important words central to mankind's background, development and existence being coincidental, must be at least a zillion to one. In addition to this spelling adaptation, I have also italicised these words for added emphasis, as after a while the eye and mind will begin to see the altered spelling as normal, so the impact of these tree words may be diminished or completely overlooked.

While the interpretation of most of these word adaptations will be obvious, some may not be. To save time flicking back and forth to the reference section, from the next chapter onward, the first time a 'tree' word is used, it will be followed in brackets with the current spelling. An alphabetical glossary of these words that supports the theory of treevolution is also included in the chapters The A to H of Tree Words, The I to Z of Tree Words and the A to Z of Ty Words. In these chapters, I have listed the tree name I surmise these words derived from, the present day meaning of the word and any current occupations that are likely linked to being a descendant of that particular tree subclass. I follow this with my musings on what effects these trees may have had on our personalities and our lives.

Other than the many words ending with the 'tree' suffixes described above, there are many words and expressions in common use that have a clear reference to our link with trees. These are discussed in the relevant chapters.

The English language contains many words taken or adapted from languages of other cultures. In this sense, it could be considered a multicultural language, representative of people from many *countrees*, not just the English-speaking nations of today. This poses the question as to whether other languages contain similar references to trees. In all probability, they do, but if I delved into this to an extent where I could reach anything like a definitive answer, I would need to delay the release of treevolution by a number of years – which is time the trees and our planet may not have. In the future, should this theory be transcribed into different languages, I believe we will find a similar pattern that will add further credibility to this work.

Our language is constantly changing and evolving. New words come into vogue all the time. Old words fall by the wayside and eventually disappear from everyday use to inevitably languish in old dictionaries, filed away in the seldom-visited recesses of aging libraries. The interpretations of words often take on altered meanings. For example, when I was young and someone asked to borrow something, there was the implication that the 'something' would be returned in a timely manner and in the condition it was borrowed. Nowadays, when someone asks to borrow whatever, you always have the feeling it's the last time you will see it! Some words now have totally new meanings, particularly since the advent and proliferation of computers and mobile phones, which has happened over such a short period of *histree*. When I went to school, a mega-bite was something you did to your school lunchbox sandwich and a terra-bite was only a rare occurrence that happened if you got lucky (or unlucky, depending on who was involved) at a Dracula party! Then there are some words in need of being reinterpreted to a meaning more relevant in today's world. For example, the word oxymoron, meaning two words or phrases used together that have or seem to have opposite meanings, would make more sense if it described an incompetent welder. Significantly, over time, the spelling of many words has altered, and this has been the smokescreen hiding this discovery until now.

Before we look at all of the 'tree' words and their links to humans, it is important to establish the theory's credibility by looking for clues as to how this English-language connection between us and trees could have occurred. To do this, it is necessary to delve into evolutionary history. I trust the next 6 short chapters are sufficient for this or to at least open one's mind to its possibilities. These chapters will then be followed by The Nature of Trees and a series of chapters that look into the close relationships between humans and trees.

TREEVOLUTION AND EVOLUTIONARY THEORY

∙∙∙∙∿∙✦∿∙∙∙∙

I t would not be appropriate to publish a work asserting that human origins are linked to trees without acknowledging and considering currently accepted evolutionary theory. Additionally, it is important to identify where we have agreement and where I see divergence.

It is generally accepted by evolutionists that humans are direct descendants of primates. With ninety-nine per cent of our genetic make-up being the same as our nearest cousins, it is difficult to argue against this point of view. Debate still rages as to the time when humans last had a common ancestor with primates, with 5–8 million years ago being the general consensus. Agreement as to which lineage of primate we came from is also debatable, with chimpanzees and bonobos championed by most palaeontologists, while others favour one of several species of great apes living at the time.

Current evolutionary theory suggests our early primate ancestors began migrating out of Africa to Asia and then to Europe about 2 million years ago. To me, it is here that current thinking becomes somewhat tenuous. If all humans on earth are descended from primates originating from Africa, how did these primates get to South America some 2 million years ago, over a distance in today's world of 2,839 kilometres across the Atlantic Ocean?

One explanation that offers a simple answer is that eons ago, Africa and South America were joined together in one large landmass called Gondwana (a supercontinent consisting of the following present-day land masses: Africa, South America, India, Madagascar, Australia, New Zealand and Arabia). This would have allowed the primitive human precursor species from the old world (Africa) and primates of the new world (South American) to have easily moved from one region to another.

However, more recent modelling, using molecular clock estimates, suggests there was a one-hundred-million-year gap between when the land masses of Africa and South America began drifting apart, and the dating of the last common ancestor for new and old-world primates in South America. This more credible information effectively rules out a direct-route land crossing. With that scenario debunked, another plausible explanation was needed for evolutionary theory to maintain credibility.

The possibility that primates came from other land routes, such as via Antarctica and down through North America, is not supported by any findings of fossil remains. Given that the search for primate remains is understandably a key area of research interest for humans, and the most recorded, this lack of any evidence to support a land crossing has left evolutionists with just one tenuous, mind stretching explanation – the primate ancestors of humans sailed across the Atlantic Ocean from Africa about 40 million years ago!

In essence, to preserve the validity of current evolutionary thinking, it is essential to think that a very long time ago, a group of male and female primates on a beach in Africa, bored with a life of plenty, decided to venture out to sea on some form of crude floating structure for a bit of adventure. After an estimated time of around sixty days (factoring in favourable winds and tidal currents, and of course, no storms) with little to no food or water and spent totally exposed to the elements, they just hopped off on to a nice sandy beach in South America and began procreating across the continent! Even allowing for global land mass movement over the past 40 million years, when the continents of Africa and the Americas were closer together than today, these intrepid seafaring primates would still have had to 'sail' across 1,500–2,000 kilometres of dangerous ocean.

And I was apprehensive in thinking my theory of treevolution would be a bit of a mind stretch! By this standard, it's not anymore.

It has always puzzled me as to how and from where the various races of humanity came. To suggest the differences – particularly in facial features, skin colour, and body size and shape – have all come from one species from Africa has several flaws, the main one being the tenuous explanation as to how these primates managed to migrate from Africa to the American continent.

If we dismiss the highly improbable primate sea journey theory and accept that all primates from which humans evolved came from Africa, the question still remains: how did all those other unique primates (and probably other animals that are different species from those in Africa), come to be on the American continent? I cannot see many of the following South American mammals surviving such a sea journey: capybaras, tapirs, giant anteaters, llamas, alpacas, agoutis, vicunas, chinchillas, cougars, opossums, ocelots and guanacos – just to name a few.

The point of this is that mammals were likely to have been evolving on totally disconnected land masses worldwide at around the same time, so there is no reason to suggest this could not also have led to the independent evolution of primates in South America. This then raises the distinct possibility, if not probability, that humans would have evolved from South American primates in similar ways to those in Africa, thus leading to the evolution of all early humans in South and North America. Similarly, it is likely that the peoples of Asia and Europe are descended from primates that continued to evolve independently from those in Africa. This proposition is supported by the findings of 1990s researchers when assessing the remains of small, squirrel-sized primates that lived 37–45 million years ago in China, Myanmar and other Asian nations, as well as western North America.

This hypothesis could explain these physical differences in modern humans, thereby eliminating the need for evolutionists to cling to this tenuous argument about a highly improbable primate Atlantic Ocean crossing.

However, if all humans did evolve only from African primates, there are several logical ways in which they could have come into being elsewhere on our world.

The first involves the same theory of an ocean crossing from Africa to South America, but instead of primates making the trip, a floating structure, probably consisting of vegetation and timber thrown together in a storm, may have carried the seeds of the same species of trees old-world monkeys evolved from. When this structure found its way to South America, the seeds found fertile ground and re-established the same cycle of evolution that produced the lineage of primates and other mammals as occurred in Africa.

The second possibility is that tree seeds were transported by *migratree* (migratory) birds, not intentionally, but because the birds ingested them not long before they left Africa to fly to South America. On arrival at their destination, the birds, having digested the outer coating of either tree nuts or fruits consumed just prior to their departure from Africa, could have excreted the seeds and let nature take care of the rest. Whether or not the seeds of these trees came from seeds washed ashore from birds excreting mid-flight or from excretia released once they landed may always be a *mystree* (mystery).

If this sounds a bit far-fetched, consider the longest recently confirmed non-stop flight of a female bar-tailed godwit, tracked by biologists using satellite tags. This bird flew at least 13,560 kilometres from Alaska to New Zealand without a break, flying for just over eleven days. There are many other current-day bird species that make flights over such long distances, so it is not unreasonable to suggest that 40 million years ago, there would have been birds that could at least make a sea crossing of about a fifth of the distance achieved by the godwit. Additionally, the flight proposed above would have only taken two days for birds flying at the average godwit speed of 51 kilometres per hour. If New World monkeys did evolve from a small band of primates that somehow managed to achieve this unlikely crossing of the Atlantic Ocean, they must surely have been early descendants of *exploratrees* (exploratories).

If we accept our descendance being from primates, irrespective of which continent they evolved on and regardless of how this occurred, the most important evolutionary question that has always perplexed me is this:

Where did these primates come from in the first place?

The earliest are likely to have descended from small, nocturnal, insectivorous mammals, such as the appropriately named (in relation to the theme of this book) tree shrew, which, along with the colugo (flying lemur), are the closest living relatives to primates.

There is a wealth of scientific information that poses various scenarios to our origins, but the reality is, we really don't know. The best we can do is look at what we do know in relation to mammalian ancestry, which is the subject of the next chapter.

THE RISE OF MAMMALS

Questions abound in our desire to understand how our planet was born. Science is continually making progress and giving us new answers. Science has also provided theories as to how and why the dinosaurs evolved and became extinct. Perhaps soon, research will reveal what triggered the evolution of all the species we call mammals.

Our understanding of when mammals first evolved is still vague, with 178 million years ago being the current consensus. This theory is largely based the identification of a tiny shrew-like creature belonging to a species called morganucodontids, which was an early mammaliaform genus that lived from the late Triassic to the Middle Jurassic period about 205 million years ago. These precursors to humans first appeared 5–7 million years ago, when apelike creatures began to move habitually on two legs. Modern humans evolved from their hominid predecessors sometime between 200 and 300 thousand years ago. As to the questions of where and when all other mammals evolved, there has been a void of any reasonable explanation until now – with the theory of treevolution.

Mammals are vertebrates with the following characteristics: They are warm blooded, have hair or fur (except for whales), the presence of three middle ear bones, a four-chambered heart, a larger and more complex brain, and females have milk-producing mammary glands for nourishing their young that are born live. During the period when pre-humans were breaking away from their tree parents, it is likely they suckled from the mother tree until they evolved to live independently. Ever since that time, all mammals have suckled their young. Whether the ancient mother trees produced sap, resin or some other nutrient-rich liquid to feed their human offspring may never be known, although the burial practice in south-east Asia outlined in the chapter titled Special Relationships may provide a positive clue. I suggest scientists could unlock this *mystree* by studying those tree species alive today that produce good flows of sap, resin or syrup.

The primates other than those from which humans descended are still in a halfway stage of evolution. It is no coincidence that most are still heavily dependent on their tree ancestors, which is easily observable because most live in trees, and depend on them for safety, food and I suggest, a form of familial and spiritual attachment. They have not yet broken their ancestral umbilical cord, so to speak, and still need the security of living in or within proximity of trees. For example, orangutans found in Borneo and Sumatra, with their long arms and shaggy hair (a more evolved covering of their ancestral tree bark), may be seen to be less evolved than lowland gorillas, which are not as tree dependent.

It is likely there is a direct relationship between the word we use to describe the external appearance of a tree trunk and branch covering – its bark – with the sound primates make, that is, barking. As an aside, dogs are undoubtedly one of our closest links to our tree ancestors. Like deciduous trees that lose their leaves and shed their bark, dogs shed their hair (bark). In sheer numbers, dogs are the most-kept pets in the world, and with the commonalities we both share with our tree ancestors, it is easy to see why.

The North American genus of trees called dogwoods, could be a species from which dogs evolved. Apart from the obvious link to dogs in the name of this species, I suggest this association because of an interesting custom that was prevalent during the Victorian era. The practice had young men giving flowers from the dogwood tree to unmarried women to convey their feelings of affection. If a man's affections were reciprocated, the woman involved would keep the flowers. If not, she returned them. Could this custom have arisen simply because the young men were conveying the message that they would prefer the woman of their affections over their dog? After all, dogs have always been a man's best friend. It is a primitive and tenuous link to our tree ancestors, granted, but it is a possibility. This link with dogs to trees may also explain why dogs have a strong instinct to urinate on them. We say they are just marking their territory or leaving a scent for other dogs, but instead, could they be trying to mark which trees are their ancestors? Or perhaps it could also be a way of showing disdain for species they don't like!

At this point, it must be said that this chapter on the theory of treevolution gives some support to the existence of humanoid creatures such as the Tibetan yeti (abominable snowman) and Big Foot (sasquatch), the latter being a large, hairy, biped humanoid associated with the American pacific north-west. While it is unlikely that these creatures exist today, it is highly possible, if not probable, that they existed in the past but died out from one cause or another. On another front, I pose the question: could Edgar Rice Burroughs's fictional story of Tarzan of the Apes have some factual basis? If so, it provides a vital link in the primate/human connection. There is often a core element of truth in myth and folklore.

An unusual and unique example of the evolutionary process of animals descending from trees is the now-extinct woolly mammoth. These four-legged creatures had a thick, hairy coat (bark), were very slow moving, were very big (as would be expected from early tree descendants) and like their probable large and long-lived ancestors, had long memories. This last point is still a characteristic of current day elephants, which have common *ancestree* with the woolly mammoth. The most notable connection is what we call the trunk, which is probably the remains of the umbilical cord through which they were weaned from the trunk of their mother tree. On that note, another possible link found in the growing list of word meanings that have all but disappeared – except in the memories of older people – is in relation to long distance phone calls made in the early days of the telephone, when one made a 'trunk call'. I suggest this was so named because an elephant's call could be heard over long distances!

The most easily recognised tree-evolving species today are the antlered mammals of the Cervidae family. This grouping encompasses those forest animals that still have virtual trees growing out of their heads. Elk, moose, stags and reindeer are good examples. Their

21

branched antlers are the main characteristic that differentiates them from the Bovidae family, which encompasses all other cloven-hoofed, ruminant mammals that have horns, such as antelopes, gazelles, impalas, bison, wildebeests, muskoxen, cows, goats and sheep. The second differentiating factor between these two groups of animals is that antlers consist of dead bone, while horns are live and permanent extensions of the skull.

Zoologists attribute the spectacular protrusions we call antlers to helping males fight for their rights to females during the mating season. My view is that they did not evolve for this purpose at all, they're just in the way of the butting heads of males fighting for dominance, which is common with many other species. Pairs of male stags have been known to die after their antlers have become entangled during these fights, which does not seem to be a smart evolutionary development for the longevity of a species. It is not difficult to see that these antlers are the remnants and reminders of their current stage of evolution from their tree ancestors and they just so happen to be convenient for fighting. If this sounds a little far-fetched, consider that Cervidae animals shed their antlers every year – most tellingly – in autumn. Based on that, it doesn't take too much of a leap of logic to conclude that they are the descendants of deciduous trees. I have focused on discussing the aspects of the Bovidae and Cervidae families in this section, primarily because they appear to have the most commonality to their tree ancestors. Also, I confess to being most interested in pursuing the prospect that, with my surname, I could possibly be related to the group of animals that includes reindeer and stags. Having traced my lineage back to Wiltshire in England, I was not surprised to find out that there are still deer farms in this region. Perhaps this association is the link as to why the theory of treevolution was revealed to me. It does feel quite strange, yet at the same time, exciting and somewhat comforting, to realize that most living animals we are familiar with today are our not-so-distant cousins.

If we evolved from some tiny shrew-like creature, the question still remains as to where these creatures came from? My theory is they must have evolved somehow from trees. One line of thought as to how this could have occurred can be seen today. I strongly recommend anyone reading this to put down this work for a moment and Google 'monkey orchids.' The striking resemblance of these blooms to faces of various types of primates is nothing less than extraordinary. The chance of these plant faces resembling primates being a random occurrence would be almost non-existent. Could these plants be showing us a vital moment in the tree/plant/animal stage of evolution? They must surely be considered a vital link in the tree to mammal stage of evolution.

The final words in this chapter linking us to our tree ancestors are the two that define all humanity – homo sapiens. Homo denotes the genus or species of living things, but it is the literal translation of the word 'sapiens' that binds us to the reality of our true origins. In this word, if we make a small allowance for spelling changes over time, we can see how the wise trees have influenced the structure of our language to remind us of our true origins.

Humans are the species of mammals that have sap-in-em.

EVOLUTIONARY INTELLIGENCE

Humans are classified as one of the five classes of vertebrates (animals with backbones). Within the vertebrate category there are more than 5,000 different species of creatures classified as mammals. Of the other four categories, there are 9,000 to 10,000 birds, 15,000 fish, 9,500 reptile and 7,000 amphibian species. I cannot give exact figures, as many creatures on our planet have yet to be discovered, and species are in a continual flux of becoming extinct and doubtless, evolving. In my introduction to this work, I stated my opinion that many animals, as well as humans, descended from trees. The thought occurred to me that if the human species of mammal is the most intellectually advanced life form on this planet, it logically follows that other mammals could be expected to show superior intelligence to the other four groups.

Several studies over the years have measured the intelligence of animals in human terms. Depending on the parameters of the tests involved, the ranking of intelligence from one animal to another varies, but generally the following species are the ones that consistently rate as the smartest. Chimpanzees and orangutans are invariably ranked first, not surprisingly as we know many of today's humans are descended from them (I state many, not all, as part of this theory proposes that some humans may have evolved from trees directly or from mammals other than primates). Bottlenose dolphins are also highly intelligent and have been known to save humans from drowning by encircling sharks to distract them from attacking. Why would they do this? Perhaps they recognise our common ancestral thread much better than we do. Dogs are also high on the list of intelligent species and elephants are renowned for their long memory. Squirrels, racoons, rats and pigs are also worth mentioning on the intelligence list, as well as several species of bird, which are discussed in detail in the next chapter.

While driving over most country roads in South Australia during my working life, I saw many animals that had their lives cut short due to impact with vehicles moving at high speeds (I was trying to find a polite way of saying 'roadkill'), but never once have I seen an obviously smart crow suffer this fate. In this regard, it may take a few million or more years of evolution before kangaroos look like making the top ten list of animal intelligence.

Marsupials are members of the mammalian infra-class, Marsupialia. All surviving species of marsupials are endemic to Australasia and the South Americas. It has been suggested that the greatest diversity of marsupials is found in Australia (kangaroos, wallabies, koalas, possums, wombats and Tasmanian devils) because there were no territorial placental mammals to compete with marsupials. That sounds plausible enough and is consistent with treevolution in that this outcome would have been dependent on the tree species present at the times these creatures evolved. As there are 347 recognised species of trees endemic to Australia, it should not come as a surprise that further research identifies which of these tree species were the forebears of these unique Australian creatures.

Other Australian animals include the platypus and the echidna, which are of the order Monotremata. Fascinating though these two may be, the point here is that, despite their length of time as a species, like kangaroos and koalas, they have a long journey through evolution before they will become as intelligent as mammals. The upshot of all this is that mammals only make up about 11 per cent of the total number of creatures in the five categories, yet of the twelve species generally listed as being the most intelligent, eight are mammals (three bird species and the octopus being the exceptions). So, eighty-eight per cent of the smartest creatures on earth come from only eleven per cent of the total number. I think this validates my point. This also is the most likely reason most humans with pets have an affinity for mammals.

The relationship between various species of animals and the tree species from which they originated would undoubtedly be a fascinating study. However, that is for others to pursue with further research. What we do know with some degree of certainty, is that there are many tree species that predate the evolution of mammals by millions of years. If we accept that humans first appeared 5–7 million years ago, in relative terms, we are still babies. Perhaps this explains why trees care about us. The best qualified people to delve into this new field should be the anthropologists, whose area of expertise is human biological and physiological characteristics and their evolution.

One thing I am certain of is that my theory will generate a wide range of responses. There are still people out there who, despite the certainties we have gained in knowledge from the advances in science and astronomy over the past two hundred years or so, steadfastly refuse to acknowledge that the world is a sphere or that men landed on the moon.

I expect to see a similar response to the theory of treevolution from many people.

BIRDS

T o this point I have focused predominantly on which mammals may have evolved from trees. While the key focus of this book is the human–tree connection, it would be remiss of me not to look at the possibility that other species may also have evolved from trees. There are compelling reasons to support why most bird species would be a logical choice (the exceptions may include species such as the Australian cassowary, along with the now extinct moa and dodo, which evolved from land dinosaurs, as well as some sea birds (including pelicans).

Birds began to evolve over 150 million years ago, long before the 350 thousand years ago when humans began to evolve. The first trees (*Archaeopteris*) evolved around 420 million years ago, during the Devonian period. These early trees reproduced with spores, which limited their rate of spread, as they were largely restricted to moist locations and dependent on wind for spore dispersal. The first evidence of trees growing from seed traces back 380 million years. Seeds can far more effectively prolong the lineage of a species, first because they can lay dormant for many years, waiting for the right conditions in which to survive before sprouting, and second, because seeds can be dispersed further afield by animals – particularly birds. What better way could an intelligent tree species secure its lineage than to create its own winged farmers to spread seeds far and wide, mostly through their droppings. An example of this seed dispersal close to my heart can be seen in volunteer work I and other like-minded people do in the Belair National Park, located about 12 kilometres south-east from the centre of Adelaide. The teams aim to remove the invasive species of unwanted trees and plants, such as olive, blackberry, hawthorn, dogrose, broom, boneseed, South African daisy and Rhamnus, that overtake the native plants in this beautiful park. Many of these infestations can be attributed to birds.

If one studies the size and shape of tree leaves, it is not difficult to see that these could evolve into feathers over a few million years. If that seems somewhat extreme, I strongly recommend viewing images of the following flowers: Yulan magnolia, phalaenopsis (bird head) orchid, parrot flower, Japanese egret orchid (*Habenaria radiata*) and two Australian species: the flying duck orchid and the green regal bird flower. It does not seem statistically possible to me that the likeness of these flowers to birds could be a random event. When showing pictures of these blooms to others, their first utterance is usually 'those flowers look like birds'. When I look at these examples, I see them as pre-birds that are part way through the evolutionary process to becoming the living creatures we recognise today. I realise this example involves plants (specifically epiphytes)[1], which are not trees, but it could be a significant step in the chain of evolution. If this is possible, it raises the credibility of similar evolutionary processes enabling birds and other creatures to evolve from trees.

Most of us know that birds can communicate with birds of the same species, forage for food, court and breed, and live mostly in trees. They are also often attractive to look at, marvellous to watch in flight and occasionally annoy us with their noisy calls and the occasional plop on the outdoor furniture. Generally, in so far as intelligence goes, it is my opinion that most people would rate birds well down in a list of other creatures. There is strong bias to confirm this in the term 'bird brain', a less than *complimentree* (complimentary) statement, if ever there was one. This jaundiced view of birds' intelligence isn't helped by the knowledge that birds, pro-rata to body size and weight, have much smaller brains than other animals – particularly mammals. However, researchers are now revealing examples of fascinating strategies and degrees of intelligence in birds that most would consider to be uniquely human. Acts of deception, manipulation, cheating, kidnapping and even infanticide, balanced with acts of cooperation, collaboration, altruism, culture and play are certainly not types of behaviours most would associate with birds.

---

1 Epiphytes are plants that grow on the surface of another plant. They do not take nutrients from the host but absorb their needs from the air, rain and decaying matter around them.

In recent years, many preconceived beliefs about bird behaviour have been debunked. Several sources have contributed to this, such as the use of technology to film bird behaviour, miniature tracking devices to study *migratree* (migratory) habits, and the use of the internet to disseminate and share information with like-minded researchers.

Brain size is not necessarily a good marker for intelligence, particularly when it comes to birds. This should not come as a surprise today, as anyone who has ever taken a sim card out of their phone would be aware of just how much information can be stored in such a small, lightweight object. The evidence is forcing us to change our understanding of birdlife as many perceive it to be, based on limited human senses, blinding biases and preconceptions as to what birds are and do.

There are four key points in this chapter arising from what may appear to be a disproportionate amount of focus on birds over the generally more-studied mammals. The first is to highlight the evidence of intelligence in trees that adapted to their grounded existence and evolved a strategy of survival by creating an army of winged servants to disperse the seeds of their species. In exchange, the trees often provided the birds with food and a safe refuge from ground-dwelling predators. If trees could do this, the probability that they could give life to other creatures over the next 150 million years must be given credence.

The second point is to show how much closer birds are to being like us than most people would have thought possible, thereby adding credibility to my suggestion that they, along with humans and most mammals, are tree descendants. For anyone interested in finding out more about bird behaviours that parallel the gamut of human interactions, I suggest reading Jennifer Ackerman's work, *The Bird Way: A New Look at How Birds Talk, Work, Play, Parent, and Think*. My third point is this: none of these new discoveries about birdlife would have come to light if people had not been searching for it, so if we had enough people and resources to look at and study trees from a new perspective, what exciting *mystrees* might we discover about human and animal relationships with them?

Finally, I pose this key observation – of the tens of thousands of living creatures on this planet, only two habitually walk upright on two legs – humans and birds.

THE THEORY OF TREEVOLUTION AND THE FIRST AUSTRALIANS

The theory of treevolution's most contentious deviation from accepted evolutionary thinking is the possibility that some humans and other animal species may have descended from mammals other than primates. Indeed, some may have bypassed the primate–mammal link entirely by descending directly from trees. If that sounds incredulous, consider the possible origins of the oldest living culture on earth, the First Australians. Scientific evidence points to humans living in Australia for at least 60,000 years, even though humans only developed the means to travel across the vast oceans in enough numbers to populate new lands in the past few thousand years or so.

As Australia has always been an island, at least in human times, it is highly improbable the First Australians could have come across land to get here. That leaves the option of them coming by sea, presumably from Timor in the Indonesian archipelago (a distance of some 90 kilometres) or possibly New Guinea (a distance of 157 kilometres between the nearest points), some 30,000 years before archaeological records show that humans could migrate in this way from anywhere on the planet.

Remains found in Tasmanian caves indicate human occupation there at least 35,000 years ago. Tasmania is 240 kilometres from the nearest point of mainland Australia. How did they get there? If it was by boat, the question must be asked, 'Why would anyone with half a brain decide to set out to sea on a dangerous passage across Bass Strait to a potential landmass that would obviously be a lot colder than mainland Australia?' It doesn't make much sense. The only explanation I have found for human's inhabiting Tasmania is that they 'walked' across from the mainland about 30,000 years ago (which is 5,000 years after evidence has shown humans living in Tasmania), after an ice age caused the oceans to recede more than 120 metres, exposing the sea floor between Tasmania and the mainland. Then, the First Australians who crossed to Tasmania became isolated after the ice melted, refilling Bass Strait, over the next 6,000 years. While this may have been possible, this scenario seems to be as improbable as the explanation as to how ancient primates migrated to the Americas from Africa.

The theorised remarkable sea voyages allowing human recolonisation in new lands would have required vast intellect, skills and knowledge. Surely if people had made such evolutionary progress 60,000 or so years ago, these people would have continued to migrate to the point where they may have colonised much of the Pacific region by the time European explorers began to explore our region of the world. As this is not the case, there must be other reasons as to how they came to be here. The search for primate remains worldwide is understandably a key area of research interest for humans and the most recorded. Despite this, there is not a shred of evidence that primates ever existed in Australia, so it is unlikely that First Australians could have evolved from that source.

It is becoming increasingly accepted in scientific circles that Australia has some of the most ancient rainforests on Earth, which teem with primitive plants and trees. This invites the distinct possibility of finding the link for the evolution of the First Australians and many of Australia's unique animals and birds to endemic Australian trees. I feel certain that dendrologists will eventually identify some of the 347 native Australian tree species as the true ancestors of kangaroos, koalas, wombats, bandicoots and other mammals found in this remarkable *countree*.

It is also likely that some species of trees with genetic links to their human descendants are still living today. With regard to the First Australians, the link to their origins may be revealed by studying the Bunya pine (*Araucaria bidwillii*), which is native to Queensland. This genus was widespread in both the northern and southern hemispheres during the Jurassic and Cretaceous periods. Now, its growth is restricted to the Bunya Mountains in south-eastern Queensland (a subtropical area of cool green forests, eucalypt forests and woodlands), and two small areas in the world-heritage-listed wet tropics of north-east Queensland.

I have suggested this species as the most likely to study for three reasons.

Firstly, the species existed when dinosaurs roamed the earth, so they preceded humans by a very long time. Secondly, it sprouts huge 20–30-centimetre-wide cones that weigh up to 10 kilograms, which would have provided a good food source for their early human offspring. Thirdly, *histree* confirms a special relationship between these trees and many First Australians. Different Aboriginal nations have been known to travel from Queensland and New South Wales to the Bunya Mountains to feast on the Bunya nuts, as well as meet to discuss trade, grievance issues and marriages. Mirroring the Chipco movement in India (refer to chapter Humans and Trees), First Australians fiercely protected the trees in the early days of colonisation, eventually leading to a colonial ban on them being cut down. Today, many First Australian groups including the Wakawaka, Githabul, Kabikabi, Jarowar, Goreng Goreng, Butchulla, Quandamooka, Burangam, Yiman and Wulili tribes still have strong cultural and spiritual connections to the Bunya Mountains.

Additionally, what initially drew my interest to this tree was a particular feature of its appearance. Call it a hunch, a delusion or what you will, but the marks left on the trunk when lower branches come away look like ancient mammal teats, as though they are the remnants of having suckled offspring (and just in case you are thinking it, I do not suffer from dendrophilia, which, if you are unaware of it, is discussed in the chapter The Theory of Treevolution and Sex). Another tree with similar mammalian characteristics is the monkey puzzle tree (*Araucaria araucana*), native to central and southern Chile, and western Argentina. I was interested by the common name, thinking this could be a link in the relationship of trees to primates in Australia, which could well void my whole premise that the First Australians did not evolve from primates. I was relieved to find the name came from a chance remark from an Englishman a couple of centuries ago, when he apparently commented that it would need a monkey to figure out how to climb to the top of such a tree. This somehow took root, and the description stuck.

Related to Bunya trees, the origin of the monkey puzzle tree can be traced back to about 200 million years ago. These trees can live for a thousand years, grow to 150 feet tall and produce coconut-sized pinecones, which hold almond-sized seeds. As with Bunya nuts, these seeds are edible. Interestingly, these trees are either male or female, with the occasional tree being a hermaphrodite, enabling it to produce cones from both sexes. It does not require much imagination or reasoning to see parallels with how these sexual natures manifest in humans.

A third Australian species that may be linked to First Australian is the Wollemi pine (*Wollemia nobilis*), one of the world's oldest and rarest species, known to have covered much of the Australian continent 100 million years ago. Related to both the Bunya and monkey puzzle trees, it was thought to have been extinct millions of years ago. However, in 1994, a field officer, David Noble, made a chance discovery of some of these trees growing in the Wollemi National Park (from which the tree derives its name) in New South Wales, less than 200 kilometres from Sydney. Growing to similar sizes as the Bunya and monkey puzzle trees, there are currently fewer than 100 Wollemi pines growing in the wild. Although I have not been able to trace any information linking the First Nations peoples to this tree species, the fact they still exist suggests they may have been more widespread 45,000 years ago and presents a definite possibility they are distant forebears of the First Nations Australians.

I realise what I am proposing here will be seen by many as ridiculous, impossible, outrageous, possibly racist and a whole lot more, but before making judgements, consider the following. If we look at the mythology of ancient civilisations – from North and South America, Europe, Asia and Africa – one type of creature is fundamental to them all: snakes or serpents. For example, in Chinese mythology, the woman-headed snake, Nuwa, made the first human from clay. In Greek cosmological mythology, Ophion the snake incubated the primordial egg from which all created things were born. In other cultures, snakes symbolise the umbilical cord. According to The Dreaming (the belief system of the First Australians), the land and people were created by spirits, many of them being animal spirits, including huge snakes. Just what triggered this commonality across multiple ancient cultures may always remain a *mystree*, but whatever the causative effects or exact timing were, does not change the reality of what happened to enable us to be here today. In myth, there is often a core element of truth.

Billions of dollars have been spent on space exploration in a quest to solve the *mystrees* of our planet and the universe. Looking at our world in a different way, such as by putting more effort into studying ancient history closer to home, could reveal some amazing truths as to the origins of the different human races. What better place to start than with the world's oldest surviving culture, the First Australians?

In summary of the last five chapters, Treevolution supports current evolutionary theory in that some humans evolved from African primates. As to the question of humans evolving in the Americas and probably other regions of the world, it is quite probable they evolved from primates at a similar time and by the same evolutionary process, yet independently from those that evolved in Africa. The major deviation from accepted evolutionary thinking, and no doubt the most contentious, is the possibility that some humans may have descended from animals other than primates or directly from trees, bypassing the primate–mammalian link altogether. Treevolution offers answers to what most would consider reasonable questions that so far do not have plausible explanations.

I can't help but feel that Charles Darwin, if he'd had access to the information available to us today, would have come to similar conclusions.

FINGERPRINTS AND KOALAS

t is general knowledge that humans and primates are linked by virtue of fingerprints. It is also well-known that each primate and every human that has ever lived, has or had its own unique set of fingerprints –much like a QR code or barcode used in commerce today.

The physiological reasoning as to why we have fingerprints is that they help with our sense of touch. While I can understand this to a point, I struggle to see why they have to be different for every single primate or human. Perhaps the answer lies with our tree ancestors. If one Googles 'tree rings and human fingerprints,' it becomes apparent that the similarities between the two must raise the question as to whether there could be a connection between primates, humans and trees. Every tree alive today, and every tree that has ever lived, has or had its own unique set of tree rings. We know tree rings can divulge information, such as the age of the tree and climatic conditions at various times of its life cycle, which explains why there would be differences in each tree's ring. But most trees in the same forest would be subjected to the same climatic variables, so I do not think they all have differing tree rings by accident. Mother Nature must have some grand plan in mind. Perhaps fingerprints are her way of showing humans they haven't fallen too far from their tree, and they need to be reminded where they came from. I believe a whole new field of scientific study needs to be created to investigate the links between tree rings and human fingerprints. It may be possible to match certain types of human prints to specific types of trees. For example, there are three main designated types of human prints – loops, whorls and arches. Each of these three patterns may be linked to evergreens or deciduous trees or possibly softwood or hardwood species.

At the end of the previous chapter, I stated that the major deviation from accepted evolutionary thinking, and no doubt the most contentious, is the possibility that some humans may have descended from animals other than primates. Bearing this in mind with my previous thoughts on how tenuously current evolutionary theory 'explains' how the First Australians came to be here, the answer to both of these scenarios may lie with the only non-primate animal in the world that has fingerprints almost identical to humans – the Australian koala.

Koalas share commonalities in physical features with primates, the most notable being they both have five digits on each forehand and five digits on each leg. Both species are heavily dependent on trees for food and safety. Fossil remains confirm the existence of koalas 25 million years ago. It is surmised they evolved from wombats around 30 to 40 million years ago and their forebears were much larger than today's koalas. These animals belong to a group of mammals known as Marsupialia, which give birth to immature young and carry them in a pouch.

Koalas 'were an important part of Aboriginal culture and feature in many of their myths and legends.'[2] 'First Australians are known to have occupied mainland Australia for at least 65,000 years.'[3] I put the words 'at least' in parentheses to suggest it may be much longer than that. 'Aboriginal people traditionally believe they have been here in their country since the time of creation and, prior to that, the continent was a land before time.'

Could it be possible that, just as modern humans are believed to have evolved from their primate predecessors sometime between 200 and 300 thousand years ago, the same process unfolded in Australia, from a marsupial predecessor?

My thinking is there would be other examples of this having occurred in the past on other continents, but the living links have long gone, as the originating mammalian species has become extinct for one reason or another – climatic and environmental changes and diseases

2 Australian Koala Foundation. *History of Koalas*, savethekoala.com/about-koalas/history-of-koalas/
3 National Museum of Australia. *Evidence of First Peoples*. www.nma.gov.au/defining-moments/resources/evidence-of-first-peoples

being some of the key ones. The number one cause for extinction would probably have been caused by apex predators. It is a strange paradox that Australia is known to contain more creatures that can kill or severely harm humans than any other continent in the world, but we are unique in that we do not have any large apex predators, and this has enabled many Australian mammals to survive until now.

That said, the koala was almost wiped out less than a hundred years ago by the cruellest predator on the planet – humans. With the arrival of Europeans in Australia came the clearing of forests for farming and timber, resulting in habitat losses for koalas and other native animals. Additionally, Koalas, were quickly identified as being a source of fur for trade. In the ensuing years up until the 1930s, millions of koalas were shot for their pelts. In 1919, the Queensland government announced a 6-month open season on koalas. In that period alone, one million of these defenceless animals were estimated to have been killed. By 1924, koalas were extinct in South Australia, severely depleted in New South Wales and population estimates for Victoria were as low as 500. Fortunately, public outrage at the slaughter forced governments in all states to declare the koala a protected species by the late 1930s. Unfortunately, no laws have been brought in to protect the gum trees koalas rely upon for their food and shelter.[4]

Amnesty International reports that 'there are around 476 million indigenous people around the world, incorporating over 5,000 different cultural and ethnic groups and more than 4,000 different languages from 90 countries.'[5] Could some of these groups be similarly linked to species of mammals (most, if not all of which are probably extinct) other than primates?

Throughout the course of human *histree*, great civilisations have been built, thrived and then declined. Many of these are well documented by historians, but others just seem to have disappeared, leaving few clues as to what caused their demise. Some of those we know about include the Mayans, Incas and Aztecs of the South

4 Australian Koala Foundation. *History of Koalas*, savethekoala.com/about-koalas/history-of-koalas/
5 United Nations. *Indigenous Peoples: Respect NOT Dehumanization*. www.un.org/en/fight-racism/vulnerable-groups/indigenous-peoples

Americas, the Khmer Empire in Cambodia, the Mississippians of the American south-east and mid-continent, the Indus civilisation of India, Pakistan and Afghanistan, and the Polynesians of Easter Island. Could the peoples of these civilisations have evolved from mammals other than primates? Perhaps anthropologists and archaeologists could research endemic animals that lived in these areas thousands of years before these civilisations flourished.

So, I pose this question – could this cute, cuddly, tree-climbing koala be a key link in the evolution of the First Australians? If this could be proven, or at least viewed as possible, it would open up a new branch of anthropology to study other possible human connections with either living or extinct mammals. It is my hope that a positive light will benefit all First Nations People as an outcome of this.

It is now time to turn our attention to some known facts about trees, to enable us to understand how they could be related to humans.

***

THE NATURE OF TREES

What would our world be like without trees? In practical terms, trees provide us with shade, food (fruits and nuts), timber, resins, varnishes, glues, dyes and paint, gums of many kinds, fibres, and most importantly, paper. How on earth would we have survived the coronavirus pandemic without toilet paper? Most importantly, without timber, the ships that played an essential role in changing the course of the world would never have been built. The list is as obvious as it is endless.

However, it is the intangible effects of how and why trees make us feel and act as humans that is a key focus of this book. Before looking at specific sections devoted to how trees influence areas of human life, it is important to begin to understand them by looking at some known tree facts. Once we begin to accept the commonalities between tree and human behaviour, it will be easier to embrace the validity of treevolution and hopefully ease your mind that I am not 'barking up the wrong tree', so to speak.

With all the high-tech facilities at our disposal today, it may come as a surprise to learn that no-one really knows just how many species of trees exist on our planet. The consensus amongst botanists worldwide is that there are about 60,000 species. Estimating just how many individual trees there are in total is much more difficult. The best information I could find, in *Mapping Tree Density at a Global Scale*[6], puts the number at 3.04 trillion. If, like me, you find the concept of trying to grasp the scale of a number one followed by twelve zeros beyond comprehension, it may be easier and somewhat more comforting, to comprehend this statistic as being about 400 trees per person on Earth (based on a population estimate of 7.53 billion people). What is less comforting to realise is that each year, about 15 billion trees are lost to human actions. This sobering estimate brings remaining worldwide numbers down to

---

6 TW Crowther, et al. (2015). Mapping Tree Density at a Global Scale. *Nature*, 525(7568), 201–205.

52 per cent of what covered the earth only 2 centuries ago, when the human population was about one billion. To put this loss into some kind of visual perspective, each year, worldwide, we are losing forested areas equivalent to the entire size of Britain. Research from the World Wildlife Fund 'estimates that deforestation could result in the loss of up to 28,000 species by 2050, causing disruption to ecological balance and undermining ecological resilience.'[7]

Trees in a natural setting have never had an easy life. The seed from which they grow has no choice in where it lands, and few situations provide the ideal conditions for them to grow. From the moment a seed germinates to the time the tree eventually dies, it must compete for water, nutrients, sunlight and space. It must also endure extremes in temperature, attacks from parasites, and depending on location, floods, droughts and fires. A long-lived oak tree can produce up to 10,000 acorns in a mast year (a year that produces more than an average yield) and more than 10 million in a lifetime. Yet, of all these acorns, it is likely only one will survive long enough to replicate the lifespan of the parent tree. Considering these statistics and in relation to my theory that we are descended from trees, it is a tragic irony that humans are their main threat. Life can be as tough for a tree as for any other living creature.

So, what do they do to survive?

To begin with, it is now known that trees can communicate with each other. In this way, information about insects, moisture conditions and relevant threats can be shared. One way some species do this is by passing chemical compounds and electrical impulses through their roots, albeit at a snail's pace of about a centimetre a second. This may seem painfully slow, but even at this rate it would not take long (in tree terms) to extend through the whole tree, from the roots, up through the branches and into the foliage. Some tree species are known to have a sense of smell they use for communication. For example, an African acacia being chomped on by a giraffe releases ethylene, which wafts to

7 Evertreen (2024). *How Many Trees Do We Cut Down Every Year?* www.evertreen.com/news/how-many-trees-do-we-cut-down-every-year

neighbouring trees, warning them danger is near. The trees can't very well take flight, but they immediately begin producing chemicals to send up to their leaves. It is not clear whether these chemicals produce an unpleasant taste or invoke sickness, but the giraffes instinctively know what is happening and move away to nibble on trees well away from those that have been forewarned of their presence. A similar process occurs when trees are attacked by leaf-eating insects. The difference here is that the trees produce a chemical signal to attract other insects that will feed on the insects attacking the tree. Apparently, the trees 'taste' the saliva of the particular pest and respond accordingly.

Most interestingly (or should I say, tellingly) in relation to my theory, recent research shows forest trees have established social networks. Because mature forest-tree roots extend underground over a space more than twice the area of their crown, they intersect and grow into one another. Apart from the interactions just mentioned, trees share nutrients and communicate with each other via soil fungi that connect the soil and vegetation in a weblike matrix. In a very real sense, trees can care for each other. They share food, not only within the same species, but also with other species. This interconnectivity has developed because trees, particularly in a forest environment, need each other for survival. Trees use electrical activity as part of their communication strategies, have a sense of smell, can 'taste' through their leaves, can learn, have memory, make decisions and grow best when they band together as communities. Plants emit sounds and hear others, which guide them to modify their behaviour.[8] Surely this must raise the possibility they could communicate with us and also evolve into other species of intelligent life.

A key platform of this theory is based on the assertion that trees have influenced the development of the English language in order to communicate with humans. Therefore, it is appropriate to look at any evidence showing that this has occurred. One of the earliest indications that plants can communicate with us was revealed in the 1960s, when an American, Cleve Backster, a well-known lie detector

---

8   Monica Gagliano (2018). *Thus Spoke The Plant: A Remarkable Journey of Groundbreaking Scientific Discoveries and Personal Encounters with Plants*. North Atlantic Books.

exponent of the times, decided on a whim, to attach a lie detector to a plant (described as *dracaena massangeana*) in his office. He wondered if anything would be detected if he burned a leaf. The instant he had this thought, even before he could consider how he would burn the leaf, the lie detector made an unusual pattern on the tracing paper. After checking that the instrument was functioning correctly, he concluded the plant had read his mind. With help from his colleagues over the next several years, he ran hundreds of tests on more than 25 plant varieties. He showed that plants have a memory for different people and can read the minds of their caretakers, even from thousands of kilometres away. He conducted interviews with people, instructing them to lie part of the time, and the plants told him when they were lying. His work led to his theory of primary perception, where he claimed that plants feel pain and have extrasensory perception, confirming that plants are much smarter than we think.

Not surprisingly, Backster's work has been discredited and rejected by the scientific community. I cannot help but feel he will be remembered in a much more positive way as more light is shone on this human/plant interaction area of research. I hope, at the very least, that he does not have to wait as long for an apology from the scientific community as it took for Galileo to receive the same from the Catholic Church. On 13 October 1992, Pope John Paul 11 made a formal apology for Galileo's persecution by the church, which came about because Galileo supported the heliocentric theory (that Earth revolves around our sun), which contradicted the Church's traditional geocentric view of the universe (that Earth did not move and was the centre of the universe). This apology took 354 years to eventuate.

There are many other examples of the remarkable natures of trees and plants in the reference books listed at the conclusion of this work. I would recommend anyone interested in pursuing this topic to read *Thus Spoke the Plant* by Monica Gagliano, PhD, an Australian researcher whose experiments and interactions with plants and trees confirms and adds to Backster's findings. Her description on how the vegetal world can communicate with us is the closest explanation of the seemingly incomprehensible that I have read, '... it cannot be comprehended in a conceptual way - only the experience of feeling it (by virtue of the patterns of information that it delivers) makes it real.'

The next three chapters focus on the interactions between humans and trees, particularly with regard to the many instances demonstrating human devotion towards them. These examples of love many have for trees must come from a deep connectedness we have to them, adding further credibility to this theory.

SPECIAL RELATIONSHIPS

Most people, in addition to those involved directly through their work in areas such as *forestree*, (forestry), garden nurseries and landscaping, appreciate trees for the many benefits they provide. But for many, their feelings for trees extend much deeper than mere aesthetic and practical reasons. There are many examples in *countrees* across the world where humans have put their lives at risk by placing themselves in front of bulldozers to save a tree or two from being cut down. Sometimes it may be for a *solitree* (single) tree, but often, it's to save whole forests and ecosystems.

These people are often referred to as 'tree-huggers', a term which generally causes eyes to roll at perceived images of unkempt, unhinged, hippy types, hell-bent on stopping housing developments, mining ventures, uranium dumps or other commercially driven enterprises. Certainly, some of the definitions I found for the term are less than flattering. I had presumed the term was a relatively recent one, coming into vogue in very recent *histree*, so I was somewhat surprised to learn the term first originated in about 1730 AD, from an event in a small town in the northern states of India. Apparently, a group of more than 350 men and women were slaughtered while trying to protect the trees in their village from being cut down and used to build a palace. These people, known as Bishnois (from their beliefs in a branch of Hinduism), considered the khejri trees in their villages to be sacred. In more recent times, during the 1970s in north-east India, a group of peasant women exhibited the same passionate stance by linking arms around trees that were to be cut down. Within a few years this action, known by this time as the Chipko movement, had spread across India. Also known as satyagraha, the power of the growing numbers involved across India ultimately forced reforms in forestry and a moratorium on tree felling in the Himalayan regions.

In the Tana Toraja region of South Sulawesi in Southeast Asia, up until about 50 years ago, the trunk of a living Tarra tree was used as a very unusual burial site. Babies who died in their infancy were wrapped in cloth and placed upright inside a hollow carved into the trunk of the tree. A door made of woven palm-fibre threads was then placed over the opening. The Tarra tree was chosen specifically for this unique burial practice because it was believed its white, milky sap emulated a mother's milk and would continue to provide nourishment, even after death. The Toraja people believed that as the tree absorbed the child, it facilitated the infant's connection to life, growing as part of nature's natural cycle. To most people living in today's technologically driven civilisation this probably sounds bizarre, but to me it demonstrates another link between people and their ancestral tree roots.

Allied to this practice is the tradition of the Djab Wurrung people of western Victoria, in Australia. In this region is a forested area where these people meet to connect and heal. Some of the trees are about 800 years old, and they are held sacred to these people as 'birthing trees', where First Nations women have given birth to their children for an estimated fifty generations. Victorian MP Lidia Thorpe, a Djab Wurrung woman, stated, 'These trees are sacred, they are a part of who we are as Djab Wurrung people. They are a part of our survival and our story. They are part of the songline, and the land connects us to our spirit ancestors and creators. Generations of Djab Wurrung people have been born by these sacred trees.'[9] Given that First Nation Australians have the oldest human culture on Earth, I can't help but feel the connection these people have with birthing trees has much more to do with an ancient ancestral bond rather than just solely being a practical place to bring their young into the world. In relation to the theory of treevolution, the significance of these words cannot be overstated. For a number of years, the Djab Wurrung people were engaged in a battle with the Victorian Government to prevent the removal of some of these revered trees. According to the government, the removals were necessary to make way for the building of a 12-kilometre duplication

9 The Greens (2020). *Failure to Protect Djabwurrung Birthing Trees an Act of Cultural Desecration: Greens*. www.greens.org.au/news/media-release/failure-protect-djabwurrung-birthing-trees-act-cultural-desecration-greens

of the western highway between Buangor and Ararat. In late 2019, an agreement was made to preserve approximately 250 of the sacred trees, however, many more were still removed, including one estimated to be 350 years old.[10]

Another example of the bond between humans and trees is that of the Pehuenches, an ancient people of Southern Chile who lived in an isolated valley known as Quinquen, meaning 'place of refuge'. Known as the 'people of the trees', their name for the *Araucaria araucana* is pehuen. These trees are at the centre of their religion, spirituality and food source. This indigenous community is currently struggling to maintain its culture and connection to its past, as logging interests are cutting down these beautiful trees. For more than 200 million years, the pehuen have withstood the ages. Today, greed and 'progress' is their greatest threat. No doubt there are many other instances of cultures facing the same challenges as the indigenous peoples of Australia and Chile.

These are just a few examples of doubtless many others that show the deep connection people across the world have for trees and the lengths they are prepared to go to in order to protect them. Certainly, it puts a more balanced view on the term 'tree-huggers.' At the time of writing this, a Google search of the term lists more than 12,000 results. That represents an enormous number of people who take trees very seriously.

Less dramatic than tree hugging is the growing practice of *shinrin-yoku*, a movement that originated in Japan in the 1980s. Based on ancient Buddhist and Shinto practices, *shinrin-yoku* has links that can be traced to many cultures throughout *histree*. The term means 'forest bathing' or 'taking in the forest atmosphere.' Research in Japan and South Korea has led to such a volume of scientific validation of the health benefits of spending time under the canopies of forest trees, that *shinrin-yoku* has become a cornerstone of preventative health care and healing in these countries. Some of the recorded benefits include reduced blood pressure and stress levels, improved mood and sleep patterns,

10 BBC. *Djab Wurrung tree: Anger over sacred Aboriginal tree bulldozed for highway.* https://www.bbc.com/news/world-australia-54700074

and increased energy, concentration and immune system functioning. Regular practice leads to deeper and clearer intuition, general increased life force and an overall increase in feelings of happiness. Admittedly, it would be easy to dismiss these positive outcomes as the result of being removed from the stresses of day-to-day living in crowded, noisy and polluted cities, if only for short periods. I am advocating there is also a much more powerful force at work. Renowned American biologist Edward Wilson coined the term 'biophilia' to describe the intrinsic love humans have for the natural world. He suggests we have an instinctive and emotional connection with other living organisms and that there is a genetic basis for this. Treevolution proposes this genetic basis can be traced back to our tree ancestors. Scottish American naturalist, John Muir, may have been alluding to this bond we have with trees when he wrote that 'Thousands of tired, nerve-shaken, over-civilised people are beginning to find out that going to the mountains is going home ...'[11]

Another group of tree-lovers are those who are fascinated by and driven to build tree houses. At the time of writing, a Google search for 'tree houses' lists a staggering 210,000 related links. Tree houses are places of imagination, especially for the young. Authors of many children's books draw on their own fond memories of their childhood experiences in tree houses and want following generations to be able to share the same joy, freedom and stimulation of dreams and possibilities they had in their youth. A far less obvious reason, consistent with the theory of treevolution, could be that the authors' true tree ancestors are influencing their minds to create these books so that trees are appreciated, respected and remembered.

This idea that trees are subtly and quietly guiding our thoughts and emotions is the thread that continues throughout this theory. We do not know how this happens, but outcomes of research highlighted later in this book point to both the reality of its existence, and possibly how. The number of children's books relating to trees and tree houses is virtually impossible to count. A search on Google lists 1.3 million sites, far too many to single out a few for comment. The point here is

---

11 John Muir (1901). The Wild Parks and Forest Reservations of the West. *Our National Parks* (republished online) https://vault.sierraclub.org/john_muir_exhibit/writings/our_national_parks/chapter_1.aspx

that children are – to my mind – more in tune with their inner spirit and are intrinsically drawn to nature, particularly trees. Their minds have not yet been moulded by the inevitable challenges of adult life. They may be open to the calls of their tree ancestors but too young to understand, let alone interpret, what messages they may be conveying. In my own experience and from speaking to other parents, it seems we have all experienced moments when our child has shocked us with an expression or statement about something they could not have seen, heard or learnt from any known sources.

Today, there is a growing demand for adult tree houses. This is partly driven by the need to escape the pressures of urban environments that bind many of us in crowded, noisy and polluted cities. Tree houses are ideal places to rekindle the spirit of our inner child, recapturing the days when we had fewer worries, and anything seemed possible. They are places of escape that enable us to feel protected, find peace and enjoy our proximity to nature. I cannot help but feel the other reason for this demand is the subtle influence of our tree ancestors gently calling us back to be more in tune with our origins.

I would love to know how the subtle forces of our tree ancestors also influenced the minds of the screenwriters of films that feature trees, particularly two relatively recent films, Avatar from the mind of James Cameron and A Monster Calls, adapted from the book of the same name by Patrick Ness. Avatar features large 'home-trees' where the inhabitants of the mythical world of Pandora dwell. However, the 'Tree of Souls,' has the most synergy with treevolution. This tree has extreme spiritual significance to the Na'vi tribe, who believe it has a connection to Eywa, the guiding force or deity that keeps everything on their world in balance. In particular, a scene where the Na'vi link arms at the base of this tree and sway in a rhythmic ritual to try to bring one of the story's human characters back to life, looks like a replication of the underground fungi matrix we know is fundamental to the life of a tree. In A Monster Calls, I found the graphic depiction of a large humanoid tree guiding a young boy through troubling times with his age-old wisdom totally believable and am somewhat comforted to know I am not alone in my views that trees are so much more than just a backdrop to life.

J. R. R. Tolkien's *Lord of the Rings* also features walking trees that move and speak as you would expect 10,000-year-old trees to move and speak. I can't help but think Tolkien learnt more about the life of trees during his lifetime than he was prepared to divulge.

SURVIVAL OF THE FITTEST

❧❦❧

I believe the reason the English language still retains clues to our past lies in the primary force behind what drives evolution – survival of the fittest.

In all aspects of life, there are differences in size, number, strength, adaptability and longevity within and between all species. In terms of human endeavour there can be little doubt the English have had a significant impact on many cultures during the last few centuries. While they certainly aren't the only nationality to have affected cultural change in other *countrees*, I feel they have been the most globally impactful over the past 300 years. Before I continue, I feel it prudent to establish some credibility as to why the English language would be the most likely holder of remnant clues to our origins.

There are myriad ways in which we can judge the value of a country's contribution to the advancement of our world's civilisations. Art, classical music, advances in medicine and technology, for example. One of the best measures (at least to my way of thinking) must surely be sport, a civilised way of releasing the *predatree* (predatory) nature within us without usually causing any long-term harm to participants. In this regard, the British have no peer. Consider how much poorer the world stage would be today without the following sports and activities that evolved in Great Britain: football (soccer), rugby, hockey, tennis, baseball, badminton, netball, squash, lawn bowls, table tennis, snooker and darts.

Then, there are two activities so different that it seems difficult to see how they could have been imagined, let alone come into being and survive to this day. Only the English[12] could come up with an activity

---

12 Since writing this, I have been reliably informed that curling was devised by the Scots. I have chosen to leave this in the manuscript so I can provide the correction and enlighten others who may be under the same misconception.

called 'curling,' which seems like a bastardised combination of lawn bowls on ice and tenpin bowling without the pins and using a heavy tea kettle as the ball. Once the 'ball' is released towards its target, a couple of manic chimney sweeps glide alongside it, their sole purpose surely being to add some comedic distraction to the whole process.

The second of these activities is the gentlemanly game of cricket. I recall reading many years ago, that the English, somewhat bored with having conquered much of the known world, decided to devise an activity that could give them some concept of what eternity felt like. So, they devised a game called test cricket, which is played over five days, frequently in the blazing hot sun, and as often as not, ends in a draw. Only the tedium of time and the draining effects of the weather could have led to some of the terminology used in this 'sport'. Terms commonly used in cricket involve bowling maidens over and fielding in women's undergarments (slips), fine legs, deep fine legs, short legs and silly points. All of these suggest a short-term activity more suited to a drunken romp in a bordello than a five-day exercise on a green field in broad daylight, with hordes of onlookers watching on. There can be no doubt though, test cricket is the marathon of team sports and lives up to its name, where it challenges its participants' skills, athleticism, concentration, mental acuity and endurance far more than all games played over much shorter time frames.

In July 2022, Australia took part in the 23rd Commonwealth Games, a sporting event held every four years for all nations that were, or still are, member nations of the Commonwealth. Each of the seventy-one participating countries has had British occupancy in some manner or other during the past couple of centuries, a feat unmatched by any other nation.

The English, therefore, must have evolved from a highly advanced species of tree to have attained this dominance.

That is probably why the links to our ancestry I stumbled across are more likely to be discovered in the English Language. Perhaps the fact that during these Commonwealth Games, Australia won 67 Gold medals to England's 57 makes it only right that an Australian should make the discovery linking our common language to our true tree ancestors. I know this is a rather smug thought, but Australians are always very competitive with the English – even those of us who are not good at sport! When you read in the following chapters just how competitive our tree ancestors needed to be just to survive, you will hopefully understand and perhaps not judge me too harshly for having this attitude. Once you have come to accept the logical sequence and meanings of key words directly relating to our tree ancestors and are more accepting of this concept, we will look at how we can begin to apply the knowledge gained to improving our lives. As an example, you may well be able to work out which species of tree you are descended from based on your ancestral and *hereditree* traits. Knowing this will help you make more informed choices about key life decisions, such as careers, life partners and even which trees are more suitable for your garden to enhance your wellbeing and create a more harmonious balance with nature.

Of course, this book is based on my personal thoughts and interpretations and, as such, it cannot be an assertion of absolute belief and fact. I state this here specifically for some measure of protection should some readers think by now that I should either be burned at the stake or sent to a mental facility for a thorough assessment by a *psychiatree* (psychiatry) specialist.

This is why I refer to this *treetise* (treatise) as: The theory of treevolution.

THE MOST ROYAL TREES

F ollowing on from the previous chapter, I think it would be fair to say, that if people were asked to recall the names of their ancestors, few would be able to go back more than three or four generations. This is gradually changing, thanks largely to the marvels of modern computer technology, but in general, not many people would be able to give much detail beyond 100–200 years. Not so with the English Royal Family. Information is readily available to show that the monarchy spans 37 generations going back over 1200 years. Their longevity and prominence would suggest they must have descended from a powerful lineage of trees.

As the foundation for treevolution is based on prominent trees having influenced the development of the English language in attempts to communicate with us, it would seem appropriate to investigate if there are any links between them and members of the British Royal Family. After all, the English must have evolved from a highly advanced species of trees to have attained their territorial dominance throughout the world. If this is so and these ancient trees are trying to contact us, then it would be logical for them to have focused their efforts on communicating with the leaders of the British Monarchy.

As head of state, the monarch undertakes constitutional and representative duties which have developed over a thousand years of *histree*. They also have a less formal role as 'Head of Nation'. The Sovereign acts as a focus for national identity, unity and pride, and provides a sense of stability and continuity. In keeping with this, and the logical reasoning as to why the key to our *ancestree* (ancestry) lies within the English language, it should come as no surprise that if our tree ancestors are trying to communicate with us, they would target the monarchy with its long-standing heritage, and not the relatively short-term leaders of government. To support this line of thought, there are indications of direct links between some of the Royals and their tree ancestors. As the following shows, I suggest at least two of the Royals may know more about their true *histree* than they might otherwise care to admit.

At a pivotal point in the relatively recent history of the British Monarchy, of all the places in the Commonwealth that a young Princess Elizabeth could have been, or perhaps should not have been, on the night her father died, what would the odds be of her staying in a three-bedroom tree house wrapped around a mugumo tree (*ficus thonningii* or sacred fig) in Africa? King George VI passed away sometime overnight on either 5 or 6 February 1952, when the then-princess and her husband, Prince Philip, were staying in the highly unusual Treetops Hotel in Kenya, at the invitation of the Chief Justice of the time. When one considers the known impacts that great trees have had on other famous individuals, some of whom are detailed in the relevant chapters of this book, it is not difficult to ponder what may have transpired that night between the princess and this sacred tree. It is highly probable that Princess Elizabeth would not have been aware of what powers the tree may have imbued her with. Even if she was, the sad news she received the next morning would have brought far more pressing matters to deal with. Was this odd timing of events fate, sheer coincidence or could it just be possible that it was a pre-ordained event, orchestrated by the powers of great trees to prepare one special human to meet the challenges that lay ahead?

One thing we know for certain is that, as the longest reigning monarch, the length of Queen Elizabeth's reign is a defining testament to her adaptability and strength of character. The significance of this brief moment in *histree* was perhaps best captured in the words written by Jim Corbett, a big game hunter staying at the Lodge at the time, when he wrote in the Treetops Visitors book:

For the first time in the history of the world, a young girl climbed into a tree one day a Princess and after having what she described as her most thrilling experience she climbed down from the tree next day a Queen.[13]

With regard to this theory, I hope that at some time in the future, it will become clear that the 'most thrilling experience' part of the quote is shown to be in relation to her interaction on a metaphysical level with the sacred fig, rather than – shall we say – more earthly pleasures! I mean no disrespect here to Prince Philip.

What we do know is that both the Queen and Prince Philip have left a lasting legacy of initiatives to support the environment, particularly in relation to trees. Rather than justifying this statement with a very long list that can be readily accessed, the following examples should be adequate. In 2018, The Queen teamed up with Sir David Attenborough to produce a nature documentary titled *The Queen's Green Planet*. During this time, Sir David is quoted to have said 'Trees have been a part of the Queen's life, all her life ... join me as I take a walk around her garden, and learn of the Queen's dream of making a global network of forests.'[14] Then, to mark her Platinum Jubilee in 2022, Her Majesty launched a unique tree planting initiative, called The Queen's Green Canopy, inviting everyone – individuals, scout and girl guide groups, villages, counties, cities, schools, and corporate organisations – to play a part in enhancing the environment by planting trees. Additionally, she regularly planted commemorative trees. Likewise, Prince Philip, a noted nature lover, was an environmental activist who called attention to conservation and biodiversity threats long before they became public issues. In 1961, he became president of the British National Appeal, the first national organisation in the World Wildlife Fund family. Could this passion for trees have come from the powerful influences of their tree ancestors?

---

13 Rosie Waites (2012). *The moment a princess became a queen.* BBC News Magazine. https://www.bbc.com/news/magazine-16795006
14 iTV (2018, April 6). *Trailer - The Queens Green Planet* [video]. YouTube. https://www.youtube.com/watch?v=noX0NIGaoo0

The second example is in relation to the Queen's son, now King Charles. In 1966, as part of his schoolboy education, he was sent to Australia, where he spent 6 months attending a branch of the Geelong Grammar School, located in the foothills of the Australian alps near the town of Mansfield in the state of Victoria. Part of the reason this school was chosen was for its curriculum, which combined normal schooling with outdoor activities designed to foster initiative and independence. What would be the odds of the young prince being sent to a school named *Timbertop?* Coincidence again, perhaps, or possibly an unconscious tie to the same guiding forces that influenced his mother's experience in Kenya. Again, we will probably never know what subtle forces may have been in play. What we do know is that of the many and varied organisations and causes championed by King Charles today, those closest to his heart are projects that involve sustainable agriculture, environmental preservation and promoting initiatives to address the impacts of climate change. In a speech to an audience in Kentucky in March 2015, he said, 'If we wish to maintain our civilization, then we must look after the Earth … in failing Earth, we are failing humanity.'[15] During another speech titled *Rewiring the Economy* in July later that same year, he addressed the challenges of climate change, stating:

> *The need to join up disparate efforts on finance, sustainable development, climate change and a whole range of related challenges has been apparent for decades. But the irresistible power of 'business as usual' has so far defeated every attempt to 'rewire' our economic system in ways that will deliver what we so urgently need.*[16]

Although I wholeheartedly endorse these views, my point here is that he may unknowingly be the human tree selected by the wise trees of the world to champion the causes that are aligned with this book. His task must feel impossible at times. What he says goes against the grain of so many powerful business leaders, which may not auger

15 Courier Journal (2015, March 20). *Transcript of Prince Charles' Speech: A transcript of Prince Charles' Speech in Louisville.* www.courier-journal.com/story/news/local/2015/03/20/charles-speech/25118033/
16 The Royal Family (2015, 3 July). *A speech by HRH The Prince of Wales at the 'Rewiring the Economy'* Dinner [video]. YouTube. www.youtube.com/watch?v=ui8zj-yWaPk&ab_channel=TheRoyalFamily

well for the Monarchy as he assumes the king's mantle. I know the chances of King Charles ever reading this book are a zillion to one, but if he ever did, I would say to him, 'better to be remembered as the Founding Father of the movement that saved the Earth and humanity from itself, rather than as a short-term King of England.' One thing I do feel certain of is, if they could, all the forest trees of the world would be holding placards up by their branches, proclaiming support for their champion.

There is one more fascinating observation to be noted regarding Prince Charles, Lady Diana Spencer (as she was known before her marriage to Prince Charles) and their two sons, Princes William and Harry, which further validates the theory of treevolution. This is divulged in the chapter The A to H of Tree Words, under the heading of *hereditrees*.

The significance of the longevity of the Royals cannot be denied – they regularly outlive their humble servants, suggesting that their ancestors were long-lived trees. Everyday signs that they are true tree descendants can be seen in certain words and behaviours, many of which are rarely heard or seen outside of the Royal Family. If one ever has the good fortune to meet the Head of the Monarchy, one must learn to 'bow' in their presence. An innocuous little word, so it would seem. However, I suggest this comes from the word 'bough', meaning 'a branch of a tree.' You are literally acknowledging that you are in effect, a bough of a tree and are showing veneration in the presence of the whole, most singularly important tree, as it were.

One of the most important parts of a tree, particularly forest trees, which I believe are the most likely species the Royal Family came from, is the top part where the sunlight ensures the best growth of new foliage. We call this the crown. Of all the names one could use for the symbol of supremacy – the acknowledgement of being numero uno, number one, the big banana, the head honcho – we call it the crown. I suggest this term is used in deference to the tree ancestors from whence they came.

The links and the respect of the monarchy to the *militree* (military) is evidenced in the uniforms of the famous Royal Guards at Buckingham Palace and the service roles of many princes in the armed forces. Now I know it can get cold in London, but no rational person would choose to cover their crown with that bulky covering called a bearskin. In terms of its benefit, if there was to be an imminent threat to the monarchy, I can only see disadvantages, unless they conceal a secret weapon or are a ploy to allow the guards to capture intruders while they are laughing. The continued use of this hat can only be attributed to historical reasons, and I suggest that these are not purely *militree* based. Their continued use must have something to do with the monarchy's *hereditree histree* – perhaps a link with *sentrees* (sentries).

PRELUDE TO TREE WORDS

f we are descended from intelligent trees, it is plausible to suggest we must have inherited at least some of our talents, abilities, knowledge, thoughts and emotions from them. I suggest they are also the source of our ideas and inspirations. The verified relationships of humans interacting with trees to gain wisdom as detailed in various sections of this theory bear testament to this. It would seem logical then for trees to have influenced major areas of human endeavour, and if this holds true, it follows that these areas would have the predominant presence of tree words.

Before we move on to look at these words, I think it is necessary to see how this could have occurred. My thought process on this is as follows. Humans are basically very similar. Certainly, there are differences in some facets of appearance, but the biological functions are the same and physical abilities are comparable, as are our basic drives and instincts. Aside from cultural differences, the key factor to me as to what makes humans unique, is their natural talent to be exceptional in what they make of their lives. During my life, I have often been perplexed, amazed and sometimes envious of people who are seemingly gifted various talents and abilities or who know early in life what they want to do for a career or become in following a life purpose. It is easy enough to see and understand the competitive nature and physical prowess of individuals by reviewing the myriad range of sports played around the world. Every species of creature and plant must have such competitive traits to survive. Physical aspects aside, how and why do some people have an innate ability to become composers of classical music, great scientists, mathematicians, surgeons, writers, master painters, musicians or leaders in so many varied fields of endeavour? Is it possible that these abilities have been inherited or strongly influenced by tree ancestors? Could the great painters of the world have been related to *artistrees* (artistries), scientists to *elementrees* (elementary), explorers to *exploratrees*, mathematicians to *geometrees*, astronomers to *interplanetrees* (interplanetary), poets to *poetrees* (poetry), world leaders to *dignitrees* (dignitaries), teachers to *explanatrees* (explanatory), politicians or religious leaders to *ministrees*, and so on?

Now, imagine for a moment you are taken into a deep forest and are asked to make notes on the differences between trees. Some would be taller than others, some thicker, some may have slight differences around their roots, the bark and leaves may be different in texture and colour and so on, but in essence, despite the slight differences in their appearance, they are all trees. What we cannot see is what lies within them, just as we cannot tell by looking at a fellow human what latent talents, abilities, experience and knowledge they may have. The physical self is driven by attitudes, beliefs and feelings that may vary vastly between individuals who outwardly look similar. Treevolution asserts that certain trees possess ancient powers and age-old wisdom, and it is from these trees that we are gifted knowledge, talent, insight, intuition and wisdom, along with the ability to have empathy, be compassionate and love. I know this will seem crazy to most people. A tree is just a tree – until we begin to understand them. The work being done by those people mentioned throughout this theory shows us that we have much to learn about, and from, these sentient beings.

As to which tree types within the myriad species on earth have this power and which specific trees within the genus they are, that is a project too big for me, as it is a whole new branch of science waiting to be unravelled. All I can suggest is the likelihood that trees known as Mother Trees (as defined by Suzanne Simard's work – *Finding the Mother Tree: Discovering the Wisdom of the Forest*) would be a good point to start researching. As human talent is common among people of all races, it is likely there are trees from many species across the globe that hold these powers to communicate with us. That said, as this theory is based on the English language, a study of old trees growing in England around the time of the 16th century would be a logical starting point for research. One suggestion would be to look at the European Yew (*Taxus baccata*), a species with fossil evidence dating its existence back to 201 million years ago. Another good starting place would be the approximately 5,000-year-old yew tree known as the Fortingall Yew, found in a churchyard west of Aberfeldy. This tree could well be a link to *ministrees*. In the following chapters, when I refer to a tree as a *ministree* (as above), I am surmising that tree has specialised knowledge on religion and has the power to influence some humans to pursue religious doctrine as a lifelong pursuit. As to which botanical species of tree these could come from, that is for others to research, and this will be revealed once we understand tree language.

Hopefully, in the not-too-distant future, we will be able to provide a sample of our DNA which can then be matched with our relevant mixes of tree DNA. Every tree, if it is not a clonal replicate, has a unique pattern of variation within its DNA that distinguishes it from every other tree on the planet. Imagine the boon this would be to organisations like Ancestry.com, who currently can generate a report showing what percentage mix you have with your human ancestral lineage from around the world, based on a saliva sample. Personally, I would rather know which tree species I came from, as that is where the blueprint for my life originated.

If you have read to this point, having accepted the fact that you could indeed be descended from a species of tree and seeing the potential benefits, you could by now be feeling somewhat let down. I have built this up to be potentially one of the greatest finds to humanity, yet the means to achieving the DNA results we need have not yet been developed. However, once the world catches on to treevolution, the commercial interests of online dating enterprises and the quest of pharmaceutical companies to patent new natural drugs for all manner of conditions, should drive progress, and it will all happen relatively quickly.

It is one of my hopes that, through this work, this theory will trigger the imagination of young and enthusiastic scientists to seek the answers. There are already some contemplating this field of thought, including the Australian scientific researcher, Monica Gagliano, who in her brilliant book, challenges us to:

'... open up to the possibility that plants have some of the same senses—the ability to hear, see, smell, feel, and taste—along with distinct modalities, new dimensions to make sense of their world, such as detecting electromagnetic fields, sounds and low-voltage vibrations.'[17]

If we could study the characteristics of the tree species our DNA matched, we might be able to understand the powerful influences that subconsciously guided us to become who we are, why we have chosen our career paths and even what guides us when choosing life partners. How amazing would that be?

Knowing and understanding the origins and influencing characteristics of our tree *ancestree* could take out much of the random guesswork and stress involved in establishing someone's life path and dramatically reducing the odds of finding a compatible life partner. Let's face it, many of us, particularly when we are young, waste a lot of time and energy trying to work out who we are, how we fit into society, and what we want to do with our lives – and with whom. I have sometimes thought that many people rattle around through life like balls in an old arcade pinball machine, until by some means or other they slot into a line of work that somehow seems acceptable to them. Similarly, with their life partner. Sadly, it seems that so many people drift through life, never being sure of themselves, where they are going or what they should be doing. It is no wonder so many become stressed, confused, directionless and unhappy, with many falling into lives of addiction and crime. Some find life so difficult they take the only way out they can see, by taking their own lives. In Australia over 3,000 desperate souls take this option each year. What a tragic waste. Just as the safety and height of a new building is dependent on the design and construction of its foundations, an understanding of the blueprint of our origins should provide the foundation and design for a better human life.

What we can do is work backwards in effect, by looking at many current-day professions and relating them to their English tree-word.

---

17 Suzanne Simard, 'Foreword', in: Monica Gagliano (2018, p. ix). *Thus Spoke The Plant: A Remarkable Journey of Groundbreaking Scientific Discoveries and Personal Encounters with Plants*, North Atlantic Books.

For example, if you are a carpenter, joiner, or wood carver, you are almost certainly the descendent of *carpentrees*. As Jesus was a carpenter for much of his life, you could also have the latent talent to become a Messiah! If you work in the clothing and textile vocations, or just have a love of knitting, crochet or weaving, you are most likely related to *tapestrees* (tapestries). In time, science will be able to classify which trees have *carpentree* and *tapestree* knowledge. Through further study, we will also be able to identify which characteristics you not only inherited, but no doubt influenced your choice of livelihood and interests. Most importantly, an understanding of your tree ancestry will help identify if your work and personal life are in tune with your inner nature, which will lead to a happier, more fulfilling life. If you're not happy in your current line of work, you are probably 'barking up the wrong tree.'

To be clear, I am proposing that certain trees within various tree species have specific knowledge about aspects of human endeavour, and they can impart this knowledge and guide receptive humans towards specific vocations. In the A to H and I to Z chapters, we will look in more detail at the many and varied tree types to see which ones are most likely to have influenced your career choices. Some may be obvious, but many can be viewed in different, if not contrasting lights. After all, it is inevitable that much cross-linking of species has occurred over the past few hundred thousand years. Before we delve into this, it is important to clarify what forces may have been involved in enabling trees to profoundly influence human life.

Where did these inner forces come from? Could they have evolved in our tree ancestors as evolutionary prerequisites to enable them, and us, to survive? How could this be possible when we are talking about an organic object that has no brain or heart, so therefore cannot register thought, pain or feelings? In view of the characteristics of trees stated previously and the whole premise of this book linking our descendancy to trees, I would naturally disagree with that view. In my journey to write this theory I have gained courage in knowing I am not out on a precarious limb on my own. Just because a tree does not have a definable organ we can identify as a brain doesn't mean it doesn't have one. We just do not know yet what form it takes and how it functions. My hunch is that tree brains lie within the vast underground fungi matrix called the mycorrhizal network and I am not alone in this thought process. The term "wood wide web" was attributed to ecologist Suzanne Simard and is referenced in Peter Wohlleben's book "The Hidden Life of Trees". No doubt a Nobel Prize is waiting for the person who confirms the existence of tree brains as a key link to humans being tree descendants. I suggest the starting point for research into tree brains should start with the fungi matrix of fibres connecting tree roots with other trees.

THE THEORY OF TREEVOLUTION
AND MEDICINE

From a physiological standpoint, trees and humans have many similar physical characteristics. We stand upright, have a crown (hair or leaves) and have flexible limbs joined to a central trunk. The pattern of the bronchi (tubular branches) in our lungs is similar to the root system of most trees. Significantly, humans and trees both have vascular systems (the tubes that carry blood or other liquids). Two of the most vital functions within the human body – blood circulation and the ability to breathe – would have evolved from our ancestors' *circulatree* (circulatory) systems of sap and their ability to breathe through their leaves.

There is much in the world of medicine to support the theory of treevolution. Firstly, our blood (or should I say, sap) is pumped throughout the body by the heart via the *artrees* (arteries). It has always puzzled me that humans don't all have the same blood type. I think most people, unless they work in the medical field, don't know much more about their blood other than they have about 5 litres of it pumping around their insides; it's red; it makes a mess if it leaks out (the mess usually preceded by pain); and if we lose too much of it, we will die. If, as I surmise, we are all descended from trees, it seems logical to me that there must be a link between human blood and tree 'blood'. In the context of the theory of treevolution and for the added benefit of helping us become a little more enlightened on this rather important aspect of our health, it is important to see what medical science can reveal on this topic.

The current classification of ABO blood groups was identified early in the 20th century by Austrian physicist, Karl Landsteiner. He discovered the presence of specific types of antigens protruding from the surface of red blood cells and classified blood into the four main types of A, B, O and AB. Type A is the most ancient form and is believed to have been the only blood type in our humanoid ancestors for some time. Type B is thought to have originated some 3.5 million years ago from a genetic mutation that modified one of the sugars on the surface of red blood cells. Fast forward another 1.5 million years, to when further mutations created Type O, which has neither the A nor B versions of the sugar – this is about the time scientists generally agreed that humans first evolved in Africa. Type AB has both A and B sugars on the surface of the red blood cells. The main explanation given for the existence of the various blood types is they evolved to protect the body from attacks by foreign substances, such as bacteria, viruses and other infectious vectors.

Regardless of the blood type, the human body naturally makes antibodies that attack certain types of red blood cell antigens. For example, people with type A blood have A antigens on their red blood cells and make antibodies to attack B antigens. Conversely, people with type B blood have B antigens on their red blood cells and make antibodies that attack A antigens. This means that type A people can't donate their blood to type B people and vice versa. People who have both A and B antigens on their red blood cells make neither A nor B antibodies! Confused? All blood may look the same, but as with alcoholic drinks, it's not a good idea to mix them.

Over the last 100 years, scientists have discovered more than 20 additional blood groups. Yet, even though Landsteiner's Nobel Prize winning work was completed over a century ago, scientists still do not fully understand the function of blood antigens. If we could find links relating human blood types to their biological tree ancestors, we may be able to produce natural medications that are more targeted and effective for treating specific health conditions. The synergy of this process should also lead to medications having far fewer side effects. This process would be the medical progression of a similar practice where many people follow the principles outlined in the *Eat Right 4 Your Type* books by Doctor Peter D'Adamo, which provide guidance on what foods to eat and which ones to avoid according to blood type.

Blood analysis is already being used to confirm paternity – so I would like to think it will not be long before a similar process is used to help us trace our roots back to our tree genus. Such a procedure could encourage new areas for advancements in medical science.

The human *circulatree* system is so named because it resembles a tree. Starting with a trunk with a main *artree* (artery), probably the aorta, splitting off into main branches which have the *artrees*, which then feed the smaller arterioles and capillaries. In her book, Thus Spoke the Plant, Monica Gagliano describes her interaction with a socoba tree (*Himatanthus sucuuba*), which revealed it could be used to treat human conditions that affect the *circulatree* system. On another occasion, a tobacco plant communicated to her that it could remedy 'pulmonary conditions, specifically pneumonia,' which sounds somewhat absurd when we know smoking tobacco causes lung disease. Still, in the context of what else this plant divulged, it makes perfect sense. Human misuse or abuse of this and other plants is an indictment of our ignorance of the vegetal world and presents an incredible opportunity to change our thinking and benefit from learning how to work in harmony with them. In the context of the theory of treevolution, these examples must add credence to the assertion that the formation of all of the 'tree' words in the English language have not only been influenced by trees, but that this influence has come from trees with specific knowledge of what the words mean.

The second most vital function within the human body is our ability to breathe. Hence the importance of our *respiratree* system. From *respiratree* comes the word respiration, the process in living organisms that involves the production of energy and typically with mammals, the intake of oxygen and release of carbon dioxide, formulated by the oxidation of complex organic substances. During cellular respiration, glucose (a basic sugar derived from foods) reacts with oxygen to produce the energy needed for movement, growth and repair of damage. Water and carbon dioxide are the by-products of this process. In the context of the theory of treevolution, the fact that tree respiration is beneficial to humans and all other mammals (as they release oxygen) is no coincidence. To me, this clearly indicates trees are trying to help their mammal offspring survive, and as such, is further evidence of our unique bonds with our tree ancestors. It is probable human lungs evolved from trees with specific knowledge of the *respiratree* system.

For our early ancestors to survive, they would have had to adjust to their new-found mobility relatively quickly, so developing eyesight was essential to their survival as well as all other mammals. Just how this would have occurred I suspect will remain one of those unsolved evolutionary *mystrees*. However, the fact that the word *optometree* (optometry) exists in the English language and is the word used to define issues relating to sight would be a good starting point for scientists to delve into as to how, when, and what tree species could have been involved in this evolutionary process. In the early stages of this process, it is likely the first humans relied on taking in sap from their parent tree for nourishment while they adapted to taking in food via their developing mouths. The health of the evolving mouth was another key factor in their survival. It was most likely formed from a weakened depression, or dent in the tree. This probably explains why, to this day, the branch of healthcare dealing with our mouth and teeth is called *dentistree* (dentistry).

When looking at the base of certain trees, it is not difficult to see that our feet and toes look like the remnants of roots. The health of both would be vital to the survival of our ancient ancestors as they needed to move about to find food. This is how *podiatree* (podiatry) specialists came into being. No doubt, as those first ancestors broke away from their parent tree and began to move around, they would have encountered new challenges and biological threats. So, specialist trees called *sanitrees* (sanitaries) may have evolved to protect them from germs and disease. *Sanitrees* were probably the forerunners of our modern-day doctors. Many people today suffer from germaphobia (a pathological fear of germs, bacteria, microbes, contamination and infection from diseases) and may have too little of this species present in their biological make-up. Alternatively, *sanitrees* may have evolved as safeguards to our mental development. Either way, if we could identify which current day trees are descendants of *sanitrees*, investigations may yield medicines to help people experiencing either of these conditions.

As trees began to evolve more towards the human species we are today, they started to develop a small, oval-shaped endocrine gland attached to the base of the brain. Its function was (and still is) to secrete hormones. It is called a pituitary gland and therefore, must have evolved from the *pituitree* (pituitary). At some point in the evolutionary process, specialist trees also developed to help the species deal with growing mental and emotional challenges – hence from *psychiatrees* we now have the modern-day field of psychiatry.

Now maybe it's just me but when I look up at a beautiful tree, it is difficult to comprehend they could ever have psychological issues. As discussed in earlier chapters, the life of a tree is not easy and if we humans have all evolved from trees as I propose, then it logically follows that most, if not all, of our feelings and emotions, good and bad, can largely be attributed to our tree ancestors. Evidence that *psychiatrees* existed lies in a very small English word still in prevalent use today, which aptly ties together the relationship of a tree species to the human race – the word 'nuts.' In a physical sense, we know that many trees grow from nuts of the same species. Yet, in the context of *psychiatree*, there are many examples of the use of the word 'nuts' to describe emotional behaviour in humans that might lead to the need for corrective intervention. We have all heard terms like 'he has gone nuts' or 'he is a nut job'. The term 'go nuts' is defined in the *Macmillan Dictionary* as: 'to be or to become crazy or stupid; go out of your mind, lose the plot, take leave of your senses, to behave in a crazy, enthusiastic or violent way.' Every Australian man (at least those who aren't medical doctors) I have ever come across, refers to his testicles as 'nuts.' This raises the question, what conditions or set of circumstances could arise in relation to our nuts that would make us behave in the manner described in the definition above?

I have pondered this question at length in light of my experiences over my seventy-plus years on the planet. My first memorable experience was as a young boy pedalling furiously on my bike in an out-of-the-saddle position, only for the bike chain to snap and invite gravity to impel my groin area onto the top cross bar. There were also several instances involving a cricket ball impacting the same area at reasonable velocity and a vasectomy in later years. From these experiences, I can say I have experienced episodes ranging from severe discomfort to excruciating pain (temporary, thankfully), but nothing to make me go nuts. In fact, during each of these experiences, I was not capable of any action or emotion, other than curling up in the foetal position and venting well-known swear words that seemed utterly justifiable in the circumstances! Only when I turned my attention to what situations could have befallen our tree ancestors to make them elicit this type of behaviour did the answers became abundantly clear.

Imagine for a moment you are a forest tree in the English *countree*-side. You have invested a lot of energy producing the fruit that contains the seeds of your future offspring, but because you are rooted in one place, you are totally vulnerable to any number of potential violations: from birds, foxes and squirrels looking for a home to feed their young, to insect attacks and poor weather conditions. Then I thought about what my reaction would be if I were to be put naked in an outside area exposed to the elements, with my arms and legs pinned such that I only had minimal movements of my hands, fingers and toes. When I then imagine being subjected to all manner of creatures nibbling, biting and trying to steal my nuts … I can fully understand and respect the need for *psychiatrees*. I wouldn't just be going off my nuts, but completely off my tree!

It is highly likely that a close descendant of the *psychiatree* is the *sanitree*. We are most fortunate today in Australia, and most of the western world, because through the advances in medical science, we have never experienced the raft of terrible diseases that decimated human populations over the ages. Polio, tuberculosis, cholera, diphtheria, tetanus, leprosy, malaria, measles, typhoid, hepatitis, rubella, syphilis and gonorrhoea are just some of these diseases that threatened the survival of our human ancestors. I cannot verify this, but in a similar manner to how the Monkey Puzzle tree was named (as discussed in the chapter The Theory of Treevolution and the First Australians), I heard many years ago that the name for gonorrhoea was taken from a man who, affected by this disease and realising that he was going to die, confided to his friends 'I'm a gonner-ere'.

Apart from the physical suffering, these diseases also inflicted mental anguish and many of them could make their victims go mad. As discussed earlier, trees come under attack from all sorts of parasites and pests, above and below ground. They can't run away, roll in the grass or even have a good old scratch unless the wind blows from the right direction – it's no wonder those afflicted probably lost their sanity, albeit at a very slow pace, hence the evolutionary need for *psychiatrees* and *sanitrees*. Doctors learned long ago that humans separated from trees for any length of time can develop serious mental and emotional symptoms which often manifest with physical problems – most notably *disentree* (dysentery), which I assume is not an actual tree species, but an affliction that arose from being disassociated from trees.

Our ability to live is vitally dependent on our ability to assimilate food. This is why the *alimentree* (alimentary) canal – the digestive passage that runs from the mouth to the anus – is crucial for survival. In the early stages of the evolving human trees, much trial and error would have been necessary in finding suitable food for the evolving digestive system and so the *alimentree* canal would have often been under stress. *Suppositrees* (suppositories) were probably very small trees, or parts thereof, used to clear blockages, although how this was done is anyone's guess. Passing even a small tree through the *alimentree* canal could not have been a pleasant experience! Thankfully, today we have less dramatic means for cleansing the digestive system.

I once had cause to have a hospital visit for the purpose of having an endoscopy and a colonoscopy analysis of my *alimentree* canal in the same procedure. For the uninitiated, this means having a tube with a camera at one end inserted through the mouth (endoscopy) to explore the top part of my *alimentree* canal, then repeating the process through my rectum to explore the 'bottom' part. As I was about to be wheeled in for the anaesthetic, I asked the doctor, a well-spoken man, for a favour. At the time there was much press in the local newspapers about cost cuts and budget blowouts in the health system. With this in mind, I asked, 'If you use the same tube for both procedures, would you mind doing the one through the mouth first?' His response was not what I expected – he burst out laughing, before reassuring me they did not use the same tube for each procedure (I didn't check to ask if the same applied to the camera). I was being serious, didn't think it was funny at all and felt sure he must have had the same request on prior such occasions and was just being polite. Still, he seemed quite genuine when he said, 'That is a good one, I can't wait to tell my colleagues.' My guess is, if you spend your life examining people's insides, it must lead to a different perspective on humour. One wonders though, what would make someone decide, after years of medical study, to become a specialist in this field?

By now, you could be forgiven for thinking I have drifted off with the fairies, but I assure you there is a point in this story. I know that 'one swallow does not make a summer' as the saying goes, but I believe this is a good example to illustrate the power of our tree *ancestree* in influencing the decisions and choices we make today. I feel certain that if we could identify which (if any) trees surviving today can be identified as having *alimentree* DNA, there would be a corresponding DNA match with this type of doctor. It still puzzles me though, why they call the procedure through the mouth an end-oscopy, rather than perhaps using this word for the rectal procedure!

In traumatic, life-threatening moments, humans can sometimes become paralysed with fear. This is likely to be a primeval response where our ancient tree instincts take over and we instantly revert to become as rigid as our ancestral species. I assert it is no coincidence we refer to this reaction as being *pe-tree-fied* (petrified). This extreme reaction of reverting to the state of being stiff like a tree is undoubtedly linked to a much slower process as we age, manifesting in the condition lumbago. This is a medical condition relating to pain in the lumbar region of the back, usually associated with spinal muscle spasms, limited movement in the joints, and stiffness and soreness. Lumbar is probably derived from lumber, which we know of course, is wood.

A lumbar puncture is also called a spinal tap – a procedure to look at the cerebrospinal fluid surrounding the brain and spinal cord. My theory would strongly suggest the procedure should not be just used to check for infection (meningitis, meningococcal, etc.), but also to see if the sap (blood) is thickening up – that is, if the body is trying to revert the human back to its stiffened-tree form. While this may sound implausible, there are examples where this reversion has happened, if only partially, from a condition with a complex sounding medical name – epidermodysplasia verruciformis. Significantly, in support of my theory, it is commonly called 'tree man syndrome'. A search on the internet for 'human trees' will give examples of what may be confronting depictions of this condition. Probably the most graphic example is that of an Indonesian fisherman named Dede Koswara, known as the Tree man, because he appears to be growing tree roots from his hands. To the layman like me, there is plenty of impressive sounding medical terminology to explain this condition, which affects mainly the hands and feet. There is no cure, partly because it is relatively rare, so it does not attract the funding needed to address it, and partly because no-one is looking at the real causative factors. While most of this theory focuses on clues left in the English language to support the concept that humans are tree descendants, this condition is the clearest physical evidence for its support. I surmise that, perhaps through a greater focus on studying our tree ancestors, the real causes of the condition would be revealed, and a cure 'wood' be found!

Most early medicinal potions and drugs were derived from plants and trees. For example, aspirin was originally derived from willow trees and tea made from willow bark was known to relieve headaches and reduce fever temperatures. In India, the neem tree is still relied on to relieve pain, fevers, infections and other ailments. The Ute people of Colorado once relied on ponderosa pine for medicinal and nutritional purposes. Just over 2 kilograms of the inner bark can contain upwards of 600 calories and as much calcium as nine glasses of milk. Through modern science, we know plants and trees hold many keys to treat severe diseases. Plants have been successfully used to make vaccines against the Ebola virus for a fraction of the cost of current methods. Pharma Planter Technologies, a biopharmaceutical company based in British Columbia, developed a plant-derived antibody for HIV back in 2011 that was safe for human use. Researchers have also succeeded in developing other vaccines in plants through a process that may increase and accelerate vaccine production and reduce treatment costs. For example, scientists developed a mixture of genetic code from poliovirus and a plant-affecting virus and inserted the hybrid genes into soil bacteria. This bacterium then infected research plants, which then synthesised the vaccine, enabling it to be extracted from the leaves. Sadly, the ability to produce synthetic drugs – which I suspect is driven by need and greed – has largely pushed aside not just old ways, but also newer methods that combine nature and modern science. The more I have delved into our relationship with trees, the more I tend to think Hippocrates was right when he stated, 'let food be thy medicine and medicine be thy food.'

My final word in this chapter on the relationship between humans and the development of medicine with our tree ancestors is simply this: if all doctors would invest more time learning about effective health care by studying plants and trees, we would all get more effective *Treetment!*

THE THEORY OF TREEVOLUTION AND SCIENCE

fter the first humans evolved from their primate ancestors, there would have been a lengthy period during which vital thought processes allowing them to interpret events in their environment beyond that needed for mere survival began to develop.

I have no doubt the concept of humans developing thought processes inherited from trees may not be welcomed by the scientific community, whose stance is that a tree has no brain; therefore, it cannot register thought, pain or feelings. In view of the characteristics of trees stated previously, and the whole premise of this book linking our descendancy from trees, I naturally disagree with that view.

Consider the following words of Dr Suzanne Simard, Professor of Forest Ecology at The University of British Columbia: '… plants can communicate, are capable of learning, have memory, make decisions, and are cognisant of a greater purpose, in addition to their own Darwinian success, to the communities in which they live.'[18] Just because a tree does not have a definable organ we can identify as a brain doesn't mean it doesn't have one. We just do not yet know what form it takes and how it functions. I believe a Nobel Prize is waiting for the person who confirms the existence of 'tree brains' and hence the link of humans to their tree ancestors.

To my mind, the *elementree* (elementary) species of trees evolved to observe and study the world around them. The dictionary interpretation of the word elementary still refers in part to 'rudiments of first principles.' These were most likely one of the first species of trees on the planet to influence the development of the human brain. Their role

---

18 Suzanne Simard (2021). *Finding the Mother Tree: Uncovering the Wisdom and Intelligence of the Forest.* Penguin Books Limited

would have been to teach basic knowledge and imbue a modicum of common sense to future generations. The forefathers of all the famous scientists who ever lived, from Aristotle and Archimedes, Copernicus and Leonardo Da Vinci, through to more recent luminaries such as Einstein, Isaac Newton and Charles Darwin, would all have descended from *elementree* lineage.

About the same time, another type of trees allied to *elementrees* evolved. *Observatrees* (observatories) may have been so named for their role as lookouts, or guards for their forest communities. There may be a powerful bond between these trees and female mammals due to the needs of both to protect their young. I state this as an opinion based on my life experience of constantly being amazed at how mothers observe, sense, feel and know instinctively how to protect and raise their young. It is my opinion that if the raising of small children was left only to their fathers, the survival rate of infants growing into adulthood would drop remarkably.

Alternatively, the *observatree* types may be one of the latest to evolve, after all the basic needs of their tree communities had been met. The trees from which primates and humans evolved could not move and as far as I am aware, did not sleep (except for the cooler-climate, deciduous trees in winter) so they would have had plenty of time to observe their surroundings by day and the stars by night. Astronomers, astrologists and stargazers must have inherited their desires from some source. The dictionary interpretation of the word observatory clearly acknowledges the contribution of these trees by naming buildings dedicated to 'making observations of astronomical, meteorological or other natural phenomena' as observatories. It is likely that *observatrees* were so named because they would most likely have been trees selected to observe and learn from *elementrees*. This is evidenced by the fact that many famous scientists were also well-known for their contributions to astronomy. All the famous astronomers who ever lived, from Copernicus and Galileo, to Newton, Einstein, Hubble and Hawking, may have descended from these trees.

Two other types evolved with a scientific focus. The first of these were *biochemistrees* (biochemistries) whose interests were, not surprisingly, in studying the processes of living matter – presumably trees. The offshoot of this species were the *chemistrees* (chemistries) whose interests lay 'in the science concerned with the composition of substances and interactions'. Fast forward to the present day and we have scientists, biochemists and chemists who study and carry out experiments in purpose-built buildings called *laboratrees* (laboratories). I can only guess the function of early tree *laboratrees* was to somehow facilitate the places or environments in which the more specialised trees could operate. Perhaps they provided protection, or as the name infers, they supplied labour.

The final tree type to be mentioned in the science category are those that triggered the beginnings of mathematics – the *geometree* (geometry). These trees were concerned with 'the spatial configurations of the elements of systems.' They were probably closely related to *countrees*.

In a general sense, all trees can be categorised into one of four groupings. They are either deciduous or evergreen and softwood or hardwood. As the following chapters reveal, it is much easier to link all human behaviour and character traits to evergreen or deciduous tree *ancestree*. I had hoped that research into softwoods and hardwoods would also provide clear links to our ancestors, so I eagerly delved into the science of wood, looking for clues. I was impressed with the amount of detailed information available but became bamboozled by the technical speak, which included words such as xylems, perforation plates and fibrous tracheids which basically refers to the microstructure and strength of wood and plays a role in fluid distribution and food storage to maintain life during dormant periods. Add to this the fact that some softwoods, like Oregon, are significantly harder than the softest hardwood, such as balsa (commonly used for constructing model aircraft and scale models of buildings), and I realized I was heading down a mental rabbit hole from which I would have trouble extricating myself.

Softwood species include Douglas fir (Oregon), juniper, pine, redwood, spruce, cedar and yew. Hardwoods include alder, balsa, beech, hickory, mahogany, maple, oak, teak and walnut. Not surprisingly, hardwoods have a higher density than softwoods. There is an expression seldom heard in this day and age which may give a clue as to the tree *ancestree* of some people. The idiom 'as thick as two planks' meaning 'exceedingly stupid' may have originated as a direct reference to ones' mental acuity being associated to their hardwood ancestors. Few of us have not met at least one or two people in life, generally of the male sex, who would meet this classification. As with many areas raised in this work, this is another area of discovery ready for scientists to delve into.

All of the great explorers the world has ever known are descended from *exploratrees* (exploratory). In all probability, most humans have at least some of this explorer tree in their genetic make-up (the possible exception being those who are *sedentree* [sedentary]). Our tree ancestors would have known their human forms would need to confront very different circumstances to theirs. Somehow, whether by design or just good luck, they managed to pass down some genetic instinct that pushed their mobile offspring to explore and learn quickly in their new surroundings. Without this natural urge, it is quite probable that humans may never have survived or would have remained relatively primitive creatures. When we think of Australian explorers, most people think of early pioneers, such as Birk and Wills, Charles Sturt, Hubert Wilkins and Douglas Mawson. The powerful inner force from this species impels humans to continually seek new challenges, from the simple desire to travel and explore new destinations on earth to the conquest of outer space.

No doubt, *invent-trees* (inventory) and *industrees* (industry) are closely related, the former presumably evolving before the latter. I would have thought that the name *inventree* would imply that descendants of this tree are more likely to be inventors than take up one of those more sedate vocations linked to current definitions of this word. If so, Sir Richard Arkwright, the man attributed with starting the Industrial Revolution, was certainly one, as well as having strong links to *industrees*. Things can get squirlied up over a few hundred thousand years, so my feeling is that all of the great inventors throughout history must surely be descended from a healthy mix of *inventrees* and *industrees*.

THE THEORY OF TREEVOLUTION
AND RELIGION

Any devotee of a religious faith reading this work would probably by now have the theory of treevolution condemned as blasphemy, as it may appear that what is being advocated goes against their beliefs. Quite simply, this is not so, as there are direct links between the theory and important events recorded in the scriptures of most world religions.

In Christianity, the Books of Genesis and Revelation refer to the Tree of Life – a life-giving tree created to enhance and perpetually sustain the physical life of humanity. If there is truth in this, it is possible that Adam and Eve could have been the first 'human' offspring of this great tree, possibly a fig, as referenced in the Bible (Genesis 3, verse 7). Apparently, after they had eaten the forbidden fruit, the eyes of Adam and Eve were opened, 'and they knew that they were naked; and they sewed fig leaves together and made themselves aprons.' I surmise that Adam and Eve would not have looked anything like the fair, clear-skinned portrayals painted from the imaginations of past masters, but more like two small, ungainly, hairy-trunked trees trying to figure out what on earth they were doing – far less romantic! Let's face it, over centuries of passing down stories and information, there is bound to be a gradual 'embellishment' of truth to make the stories more palatable. Doubt even exists as to whether or not the forbidden fruit was in fact an apple.

The ancient Jewish Book of Enoch suggests that the offending fruit came from a tamarind tree. At the time, there were plenty of other possibilities: grapes, pomegranates, figs, carobs (who could resist chocolate?), pear and doubtless many others. One plausible explanation for the apple being typecast as the villain is the possibility of a verbal misunderstanding, in which the word 'malum' meaning evil, has been confused with another Latin meaning for the word 'apple'. It probably was the apple. After all, the whole purpose of eating the fruit was no doubt intended to make Eve more appealing (from the word apple) to Adam!

I also feel confident in asserting that the names Adam and Eve were not original. At best they were probably known as T1 and T2 (Tree1 and Tree2) or more likely, had no names at all. Personally, I don't buy into the whole eating of the apple with a twisted snake thing, but if there is a basis of fact in the story, it is interesting to note that Eve (or T1), apparently ate a piece of fruit – not a watermelon or a vegetable, or some wholesome grains or nuts, but a piece of fruit – from a tree. A coincidence perhaps, but if I am right, the earliest human-trees would have been very dependent on their parent trees for sustenance. The Bible makes no mention as to how and with what *rudimentree* tools T1 and T2 used in the leaf-sewing process, nor how they fared in their new 'clothes' after no doubt discovering that the sap from the green part of fig leaves is an irritant to human skin!

Can it be mere coincidence that males of later times prepared to devote their lives to protecting and passing on the knowledge and wisdom of their tree ancestors became known as *ministrees* (ministries) and joined together to live in groups in buildings known as *monastrees* (monasteries). Over time, subgroups of *ministrees* evolved to perform specific functions. Two of these are *vestrees* (vestry) and *rectrees* (rectories). Transgressors of the rules and regulations of the *ministrees* were evicted or banished into exile, doomed to perish in eternal suffering. Not surprisingly, this was called *purgatree* (purgatory), perhaps eternally doomed to one day be cut into pieces and used to build pergolas.

The Christian Bible tells us that God delivered the Ten Commandments to a man called Moses, high up on Mount Sinai. Trees live and grow through a process called osmosis. I think the similarity of this word to Moses suggests that he must have been a very important direct descendent of a most revered *bigatree* (bigotry) of the times. Could Moses have been one of the earliest true descendants to have broken away from his earth-rooted ancestors – chosen to deliver the code of conduct to the new breed of mobile human trees who were apparently losing their way on a path to sin and debauchery? Is it possible that God himself was this huge tree, the Tree of Life, rooted high up on Mount Sinai? If so, being earthbound, He couldn't very well just wander down to deliver the message to the masses, so he needed some poor sap to climb up the mountain to collect the tablets on which the life principles for human behaviour were inscribed!

There are many examples throughout *histree* of noted religious or spiritual leaders being closely linked with trees – too many to be dismissed as just a coincidence. An example of this is Buddhism, a powerful world religion originating in India about 600 years before Christ. According to traditional stories handed down through the generations, the man who would become the revered Buddha was a young prince who gave up his privileged life in Nepal to seek ways to relieve universal human suffering. After years of travelling, fasting and practising meditation, he arrived in Bodh Gaya in India and began meditating at the base of a *Ficus religiosa* tree in a quest to discover universal truth. It was through association with this tree that he attained the enlightenment he sought, and the tree became known as the Bodhi Tree. Every *Ficus religiosa* tree is considered sacred to Buddhists, but the propagation of the species over the centuries from the original Bodhi Tree are the most sacred. The current day Bodhi tree was planted in 1881 and stands by the Mahabodhi Temple, which was erected around 260 BC to commemorate the Buddha's enlightenment. It is considered by Buddhists to be one of the most significant pilgrimage destinations in the world.

The *Ginkgo biloba* species have been on earth essentially unchanged for more than 200 million years, linking the Mesozoic era of dinosaurs to the present. In the temple gardens of Buddhism, Confucianism and Shintoism, it is considered a sacred tree. Sadly, this species is listed as being endangered, with an area on Mount Tianmu in China's Zhejiang province being the only place left where it grows in the wild. One cannot help but wonder what they could divulge about human evolution if we could but tap into their wisdom and knowledge. Perhaps one hint of what secrets they hold lies near a Buddhist temple in Tokyo, Japan. There, women worship Kishimojin, a Buddhist-Hindustani Goddess, in the form of a 700-year-old *Ginkgo biloba* tree, believed to grant fertility, easy childbearing and protection for their children. Perhaps this practice is a thread indicating that DNA testing could match these women with ginkgo trees as their ancestors, providing further evidence to validate treevolution.

Histree is littered with numerous human cultures for whom trees hold deep, sacred reverence. Rowan trees are sacred in many northern European cultures, and the bristlecone pine is known as the prayer tree to the Ute people of northern America. Similarly, the Nykina and Warrwa people in the Kimberley region of north-western Australia believe the boab tree holds spiritual significance as a dwelling place of powerful beings, similar to the bunya trees in the Bunya Mountains in Queensland, as previously discussed. The Maoris of New Zealand revere the pohutukawa tree and in Japan the camphor tree is spiritually significant for devotees of the Shinto religion. In addition to the neem and biloba species mentioned previously, in India, the banyan and sacred fig are revered trees. Ayahuma (*Couroupita guianensis*) – also known as the cannonball tree because of its cannonball-sized fruit – is a tree native to the tropical forests of north-eastern South America, where it is held in high regard by the shamans of the Amazon Basin. In India, trees of this species are commonly planted as guardians of Shiva temples (I think this is used for some spiritual connection rather than any perceived effect it may have in a physical sense by using its fruit to cannonball intruders). In Sri Lanka and Thailand, Ayahuma trees outside Buddhist temples symbolise enlightenment. The Indian Sandalwood is essential to the religions of Jainism, Sufism and Zoroastrianism and to Korean, Japanese and Chinese religions.

One of the oldest religions is paganism, which generally incorporates groups of like religions outside the main religions of Christianity, Hinduism, Buddhism and Islam. Paganism is founded on ancient spiritual traditions with a reverence for nature and particular beliefs that spirits reside within trees. For example, Germanic paganism identifies nine specific trees that hold particular roles in mythology.

Germanic scholars consider that reverence for and rites performed at individual trees are derived from the mythological role of the world tree Yggdrasil (the tree of life from Norse mythology). Interestingly, latest census records show that in the USA, there are about one million people who class themselves as pagans, with fifty-three thousand in the UK and twenty-four thousand in Australia. I have the distinct feeling that most people in the western world would scorn such beliefs as being outdated and primitive, with no relevance to today's madcap, materialistic lifestyle pursuits, lawsuits and reality TV fodder with young people trying to find love wearing almost nothing but their birthday suits. On the other hand, the support for some traditional Christian church denominations is no doubt being eroded by all the shameful paedophilia coverups and goings-on that are rightly being exposed. On this last point, it may be highly significant that the word 'primate' has two seemingly unrelated meanings. The first, and most generally known, encompasses all those apes from which I accept some human species descended. The second is a title or rank bestowed on some bishops in certain Christian churches. Perhaps this indicates early links between the evolution of religion with the evolution of our human cousins from the primates of Africa. Alternatively, there has been too much adulteration of the pure *ministree* bloodline over time – perhaps with *predatrees* and *purgatrees*. Related to *ministrees*, it is arguable whether *purgatrees* were the henchmen of the *ministrees*, who hunted out the sinner trees that had transgressed goodness knows what, or if this was the name given to trees that, for some reason or other, were considered to be undesirable within the species.

A look at the number of believers in each of the major world religions and the numbers of significant trees identified as being sacred to each religion suggests to me just how in tune or not each religion is with our tree ancestors. Even though Christianity ranks number one for followers, with 2.2 billion people, it has only two trees mentioned in its teachings (the Tree of Life and the Tree of Knowledge). Although these trees are significant, they are in scripture only, whereas with most other religions, many of the trees revered by their followers are real and tangible. Islam is the second most popular religion, with 1.8 billion followers. I have not been able to identify any specific sacred trees in Islamic teachings; however, there is an overall reverence for trees and all living things in Islam's core beliefs. Next is Hinduism, with just over one billion followers and 13 identified species of sacred trees; then Buddhism with 488 million followers and 7 sacred trees; and Shintoism, with 104 million followers and many pine, camphor and forest groves being preserved for their religious significance. It seems rather ironic in the context for this work that the weakest link between religions and trees is Christianity, the main religion of English-speaking people. Perhaps, just as a splinter is a dying tree's last desperate act of revenge, my work is our ancestors' last gasp efforts through the English language to be recognised, listened too and not lost to *histree*.

To all believers in the Christian faith, I pose the following questions. Have you ever pondered where Jesus, the son of God, derived his understanding of life, wisdom and power from? Can it be mere coincidence that he spent about twenty years (Theology 101) of his life working with timber, with trees, in a humble trade of the time – *carpentree* (carpentry)?

I am including *cemetrees* (cemeteries) in this chapter as they are generally closely linked to churches and *ministrees*. Just what type of trees they could have been and why they are associated with the last resting places for many humans is a conundrum. It is more likely *cemetrees* may not have been a tree type at all and may be one of the exceptions to the general theme of treevolution that there are human descendants from all words in the English language ending in the suffixes referring to trees listed at the beginning of this work. This likelihood will no doubt give much relief to grave diggers, stonemasons, funeral directors and concreters. However, it's probable there is a relationship between *cemetrees* and cement. Perhaps it's as simple as dead people becoming hard and stiff – like concrete, of which the key stiffening ingredient is cement.

The English language has two words linked with the burial process for humans. The first one is graveyards which are associated with burial grounds in the near proximity to churches. *Cemetrees*, on the other hand are generally much larger burial sites, usually some distance away from any church and not linked to any particular religious denomination. If we look back to the earliest references to the word cemetery to glean some understanding as to where the word came from, there are two possibilities. The earliest reference attributes the name coming from a Greek word 'koiman,' meaning 'put to sleep,' and thence 'koimeterion,' meaning 'sleeping place.' This makes sense, but there is no link here to the spelling of cemetree. The other, more likely, possibility dates back to the late 14th century with the French word 'cimitiere' meaning graveyard. With the way words evolve in spelling and meaning over time, it isn't much of a leap to go from cimitiere to *cemetree*. After all, the French are pretty close to the British – geographically at least!

As cemetery is a relatively recent word, it probably came in to being as a result of either one or a combination of the following scenarios. The first possibility is that, centuries ago, small shrubs or trees were placed on burial sites rather than, or as well as, flowers. These days, if you pass by any *cemetree* you will inevitably see gravesites adorned with fresh flowers. Long ago, you couldn't just pop down to the local florist and select from a wide choice of blooms, let alone a variety of glass, metal or ceramic vases in which to put them. The limited availability, inconvenience and lack of funds to procure flowers would make a shrub or tree, probably nicked from one of the wealthy lords of the realm, a natural choice. The problem with either trees or flowers, is that they do not last long. Perhaps this led to the development of lookalike trees made from cement which would certainly last longer, thus leading to the various other adornments of headstones (crosses, statues and so on).

A second possibility may be that, long ago, there were small species of trees that grew in clay and limestone soils (the ingredients for making cement), which, for whatever natural reason, hardened like cement when they died. These were then used to adorn gravesites because they would have lasted much longer. As time passed and the supply ran dry, the practice died out, so other materials such as carved stone, granite and metal took their place. Time and nature then gradually erased all signs that the original process ever occurred and only the name endured. Leading on from the second possibility, it is highly likely that, way back in time, some trees may have grown in clay and limestone soils, and time and nature have turned those trees into the raw materials we use today to make cement, just as time turned other vegetation into oil or coal. I suggest here that it would be an interesting scientific venture to examine the tree species that live close to known cement-material-bearing areas. High levels of limestone and clay deposits in such areas could then confirm genetic links to these *cemetrees*, in which case, there would be a connection to people of the vocations mentioned earlier. Unfortunately, the only thing we can say with any degree of certainty at this point in time, is that without more concrete evidence these questions will continue to remain a *mystree*.

TREEVOLUTION AND THE ORIGINS OF ARMED FORCES

❧❧✦✐✦❧❧

I t is known that trees, particularly in a forest, are highly competitive with other species when it comes to fighting for survival – competition for space, soil nutrients, water and sunlight being the main battlegrounds. This fierce instinct was passed on to the new Homo sapiens, so it would not have taken long before different species began fighting over areas of land that were more conducive to their survival.

Specialist trees evolved and banded together to ward off other species from infiltrating their desired areas – hence *territrees* (territories) came into being. The name probably is a shortened version for what would have been territorial trees. It could also have derived from the word 'terrain', a noun referring to land, ground, topography, landscape or *countreeside*. Additionally, it could have come from the word 'terror,' as that is what they would have been trying to use to ward off potential invaders. From their ranks, they developed other trees called *sen-trees* (sentries) to guard specified regions. These evolved into the first *militrees* (militaries) from which we have the name for armies today, the military. I imagine the formation of the first *militrees* into a cohesive fighting force would have been a fairly haphazard affair. Perhaps this is where the term 'milling around' (meaning to move around with no particular purpose or direction) came from. A more gruesome and likely scenario is that the current word 'milling' – the act of grinding grain in a mill or cutting and shaping with a rotating tool – may be derived from the barbaric actions of these trees against their enemies.

In those evolving times, education and knowledge would have been very primitive, so I surmise the only way the different species could define the areas they were protecting was by counting the number of trees in their patch. *Countrees* evolved for this purpose, and I venture to say all great mathematicians across the ages could trace their origins to the tree species that could count, in whatever form that meant for a tree. Accountants, auditors and actuaries would also have lineage back to these trees. How strange it feels to know that, to this day, we still refer to the land of our birth as our *countree*, literally meaning a count of trees, in a specified *territree!*

It is possible the word *mandatree* (mandatory) came about from a generic term used to define male trees, namely man-da-tree. It is also possible that these were specific trees used in ancient times as community guards. On being threatened by invaders the call would go out to 'man-the-tree', which gave the defensive advantages of height, protection and line-of-sight. The legacy of this would be recalled by most readers aged over fifty as a military or navy call to 'man the fort' or 'man the guns'.

If this is all by now starting to sound a little far-fetched, consider the following. What do we call the winners of any conflict, be it a sporting contest or an armed conflict between *countrees?* The triumphant combatants involved are called the victors, but the winning outcome is called a *victree* (victory). In ancient Greece, the victors of sports events were crowned with circular wreaths made from wild olive tree branches. Laurel wreaths made of interlocking branches and leaves from the bay laurel also symbolized victory and honour in other arenas of *victree* and accomplishment. The Greeks were not short on their knowledge and use of metals, so why would they use this foliage over prized bronze, silver or gold to recognise their heroes, if not for the fact that, in some way, it was paying homage to their tree ancestors?

Why is the document signed by leaders of warring *countrees* who make an agreement to cease hostilities called a *treety* (treaty)?

Finally, and most significantly, can it be mere coincidence that the word reserved for the worst act that can be perpetrated by anyone against their *countree* is:

Treeson

TREE WORDS

❧✦❧

U p to this point, we have looked at tree words and their relationship to various areas affecting our lives - evolution, medicine, science and religion being the key ones. There are no doubt others, including sex, which I have deliberately delayed until later, to keep you interested! However, I trust those discussed so far are more than sufficient to convince anyone of our close relationship to trees and why they have such a significant influence on our lives.

This raises the questions: if I am the descendant of trees, which tree types could I have come from and what influence could this have had on my life? A whole new branch of science needs to be developed for definitive answers to these questions.

To me, the long list of tree words in the following chapters, most of which relate to current day vocations, suggests that our tree ancestors have been trying to educate us as to where we came from and from where our talents and abilities evolved. If this is so, the question must be asked: how on earth could trees possibly know anything about any of these human pursuits? To maintain credibility in this work, I hope the following thoughts provide sufficient credence to answer this question.

My overview of human progress is that we have mirrored our tree ancestors, in a manner perhaps best illustrated by referring to the American psychologist Abraham Laslo's 1943 'theory of human motivation,' often called the 'hierarchy of needs.' His theory describes five levels of human development and explains that one can only ascend from the base level to the next and so on, when the needs of each lower level have been met. The first level is the physiological need for food and shelter. Until these basic needs are met, along with the next stage, the need for safety (an environment in which to feel secure and protected), it becomes difficult to move on to the other stages.

The third level in the hierarchy is social needs; a sense of belonging and love. The social interaction of trees has been addressed earlier in this work. As for love, the whole premise of this book is based on the love trees have for humans. The previous chapters detailing the care and affection mammals and birds born of trees have for their offspring should be sufficient for us to accept that trees are capable of love. The fourth level is esteem; the need for status, recognition and respect. *Approbatrees* (approbatory), *complimentrees* (complimentary) and *dignitrees* are examples of trees that evolved for this function.

The last level is self-actualisation, the desire to be the most one can be. *Artistrees*, *elucidatrees* (elucidatory), *gallantrees* (gallantry), *ministrees* and *voluntrees* (voluntary) would fit this category.

I know for many who may read this work, the prospect of trees contemplating the universe (*interplanetrees*) and imbuing their human descendants with all the talents and motivational drives we exhibit today may be stretching the bounds of credibility. The remarkable scientific discoveries of Monica Gagliano, who communicates with the vegetal world through collaboration with shamans from native tribes in South America, are testament to human connection with our ancient tree roots. Her book, Thus Spoke the Plant, is a must read for anyone searching for answers to questions concerning our ability to interact with trees on an intellectual and spiritual level. Luminaries mentioned in the relevant chapters of this book who derived inspiration from trees must surely raise the credibility of this line of thought.

In the following chapters, each 'tree' word will be followed by the current spelling and definition. Bearing in mind the major context of this theory is based on the English language, it is important that the reference source needs to be a well-respected English publication. To this end I have referenced the Oxford English Reference Dictionary (Oxford University Press 1995). I have also included comments on any identifiably linked vocations and personality traits that have come to mind, and finally, any closely related species. If reading through this long list of 'tree' words becomes rather tedious, these chapters can be read separately without interrupting the flow of this work. While the urge to overlook the next six chapters and jump to The Theory of Treevolution and Sex may be tempting, I suggest the following words may be worthy of your attention before moving on: *budgetrees*, *conservatrees*, *hereditrees*, *histrees*, *lavatrees*, *monetrees*, *palmistrees* and *predatrees*.

THE A TO H
OF TREE WORDS

adultree

Adultery; 'voluntary sexual intercourse between a married person and a person (married or not) other than his or her spouse.' This word is elaborated on in the chapter on Sex.

adulatree

adulatory; 'flatter obsequiously'; fawn on.

Includes: sycophants (brownnosers to Australian readers) are good examples of those who are imbued with excessive amounts of this species' genes.

Nearest related types: approbatrees, complimentrees, congratulatrees, laudatrees.

alimentree

alimentary; 1 'of, relating to, or providing nourishment or sustenance'.

Includes: naturopaths and natural health practitioners, dieticians, herbalists.

Nearest related species: dietrees, alimentrees.

2 alimentary canal – 'the passage from mouth to anus by which food is received, digested, etc.'

Includes: specialist medical fields of gastroenterology and endocrinology, colonic irrigators and possibly sanitree engineers.

Nearest related types: dietrees, sanitreees, and possibly, lavatrees and suppositrees!

amatree

amatory; 'of or relating to lovers or lovemaking – expressive of sexual love or desire.'

Includes: sex workers, pole dancers, generally those humans with high libidos. Casanova would have been a good ancestral candidate and in recent times, possibly Bill Clinton in America and Barnaby Joyce in Australia.

Nearest related types: sultrees, perfunctrees, adultrees.

ancestree

ancestry; '1 relating to ancestral descent, one's (esp. remote) family descent'.

2 'one's ancestors collectively'.

Includes: historians, genealogists, in general anyone besotted with Ancestry.com. It is possible that there were no actual trees from which anyone has descended here. As the spelling implies, the name is most likely a general reference relating to ancient trees that were our ancestors.

Nearest related types: hereditrees, histrees.

approbatree

approbatory; 'approval, consent'.

Includes: good parents, teachers, coaches and perhaps sycophants. Good parents usually have a sprinkling of this gene to help nurture and encourage their children. Too much and you get those parents whose undisciplined bratty child can do no wrong in their eyes. These parents often lurk on committees that come up with the concept of making all kids equal winners in any activity where everyone 'wins' a participation award – another example of the changing meaning of a word.

Nearest related types: commendatrees, lauditrees, complimentrees.

arbitree

arbitrary; 1 'whimsical, random, chance, unpredictable, casual, wanton, motiveless, unreasoned, unsupported, irrational, illogical, unjustified, arbitraray. (1) based on or derived from uninformed opinion or random choice; capricious.'

2 'despotic'.

Includes: gamblers, shopaholics and some women during pregnancy. Seems to be a genetic taint in most teenagers before the hormones settle down and other dominant tree genes take over. The ingestion of alcohol and/or recreational drugs invariably override other genetic tree strains to allow this tree gene to take control of the human body and mind.

Nearest related types: lottrees, momentrees.

artistree

artistry; 'the skill of an artist'.

Additional information: To fully understand *artistrees* we must look at the meaning of the noun, artists. These are people 'who create works of art, especially paintings or drawings.' The world's greatest musical composers, painters and sculptors must have had strong influences from somewhere and this is the only tree species having a direct reference to the artistic nature exhibited in humans. The oldest known artwork, a painting of a pig in an Indonesian cave, is estimated to be about 45,000 years old. This suggests to me that our tree ancestors began influencing human creativity from about this time. Interestingly, the oldest known First Australian artwork of a kangaroo in a rock shelter in the Kimberley region of north-western Australia has been dated back just over 17,000 years. Given that we know the First Australians have an unbroken lineage of over 60,000 years, one might assume that there may have been much older findings. Perhaps there are but they haven't been discovered yet or forces of the elements have obliterated them. Then again, perhaps the unique Australian trees that were the forebears of these people took longer to influence these early artists.

Nearest related types: possibly artrees.

artree

artery; 'any of the muscular-walled tubes forming part of the blood circulation system by which blood is conveyed from the heart to all parts of the body, carrying oxygen-enriched blood from the heart'.

Includes: cardiologists, heart surgeons, phlebotomists.

Additional information: This definition points to *artrees* being one of the species involved in the physical evolution of human beings, but the descendants of these trees may have given rise to all the great artists. *Artrees* are mentioned in the chapter on The Theory of Treevolution and Medicine, and if their roots are entirely related to the physiology of humanity and not their artistic development, their probable nearest relations would be *circulatrees.*

battree

battery; 'a devise which provides a source of electric current, consisting of one or more cells for producing or storing electricity generated by a chemical reaction'.

Additional information: Since the invention of electricity only occurred in the early nineteenth century, the development of batteries is a recent innovation, so it is more likely that the name came from trees that attracted bats, those used as battering rams in days of yore, or if it is a relatively recent word, from trees used to make cricket bats, probably willows. That stated, this species may yet provide a link to show that trees do create electrical activity, which may lead to the confirmation of the existence of tree brains. As an aside, a search on the origins and meanings of the term 'assault and battery' shows it is a relatively recent term with no connection to our ancestors. However, always keen to preserve the English language, I suggest that the dwindling use of this term could be resurrected with a slight alteration in wording and meaning to be used in relation to police when they use taser guns to apprehend felons - as 'assault with battery'. Just a thought!

Nearest related types: possibly biochemistrees.

bigatree

bigotry; 'prejudice, bias, partiality, partisanship, sectarianism, discrimination, dogmatism, narrow-mindedness, racism, sexism, chauvinism, jingoism'. From bigot 'an obstinate and intolerant believer in a religion, political theory etc.'

Additional information: These traits probably arose from the physical nature of these trees being bigger and therefore more dominant in their original forest habitat. There are no real positives of the above characteristics, and no tree species linked to any specific vocations I can think of, although the general effects of humans possessing an overabundance of this genetic pre-disposition can often be observed in executives of large corporations and in government ranks (think of topical current and past leaders of the United States of America and Russia). Unfortunately, many humans today, other than as mentioned above, have varying and often excessive amounts of an ancestral mix from this species. Curiously, small dogs that try picking fights with much larger dogs often have an overabundance of *bigatree* genes, as do the kangaroos that frequent country roads traversed by fast-moving vehicles. These creatures have not evolved sufficiently to understand that this behaviour is not conducive to longevity.

Nearest related types: condemnatrees, derogatrees and discriminatrees.

biochemistree

biochemistry; 'the study of the chemical and physico-chemical processes of living organisms'.

Includes: naturalists, botanists, gardeners, agricultural scientists, lab technicians and biochemists.

Nearest related types: chemistrees and alimentrees.

budgetree

budgetary; 'relating to the amount of money needed or in accordance with an estimate of income and expenditure available (for a specific item, etc.).'

Includes: treasurers, finance ministers, accountants, bookkeepers, actuaries, tightwads and misers.

Additional information: The word evolved from French origins relating to a leather bag, no doubt so named to hold money. The leather would have most likely come from a mammal, which came from a tree, so here we can see the link that binds us to our tree ancestors through our language. Everyone needs a little *budgetree* DNA in their genetic mix if they are to achieve a measure of financial stability throughout life in western civilisation. It is easy to see the effects of having too much or too little of this tree in one's sap. Misers and tightwads (these are the ones who always pay less than their fair share at group dinners and the guy who always weasels out of his shout at the bar) have too much, whereas those who always spend more than they earn (shopaholics, those who end up with multiple maxed-out credit cards or whose concept of a budget is a former brand of car rentals), have virtually none at all. A friend who I had asked to give feedback on this work raised another possibility. His observation was that this must be one of the most ingrained characteristics of human nature and so the name may have come from the fact that these people could not budge from their ingrained fiscal habits.

Nearest related types: monetrees, repositrees and countrees.

cemetree

cemetery; 'graveyard, burial ground, esp. one not in a churchyard'.

Additional information: For reasons following, I have not listed any vocations here. I find this species to be of particular interest, not through any morbid fascination with death, but more so to understand what type of trees they could have been and why are they associated with the last resting places for many humans. It must be said, no-one scrolling through this section of treevolution eagerly trying to find their tree ancestor would be too thrilled to find that they are descended from a dead tree! It just doesn't make sense. How could one be descended from something that is dead? Cemetrees are discussed in more depth in the chapter The Theory of Treevolution and Religion.

chemistree

chemistry; 'the science concerned with study of the elements and the compounds they form and the reactions they undergo'.

Includes: scientists, lab technicians, pharmacists, munitions and fireworks manufacturers, love matchmakers, perhaps.

Nearest related types: biochemistrees.

circulatree

circulatory; 'of or relating to the circulation of blood or sap'.

Includes: cardiologists.

Additional information: The name is most likely from the trees' efficiency in pumping sap throughout its structure, or possibly the circumference of the tree, or even the inner circles that divulge the ages of trees.

Nearest related types: artrees.

commendatree

commendatory; 'serving to commend, approve or praise'.

Additional information: Most good parents have a liberal dose of this tree type in their genetic make-up, as do members of the Monarchy who bestow various awards and the occasional knighthood from time to time. These trees probably evolved to balance the negative impacts of *condemnatrees*.

Nearest related type: approbatrees, lauditrees.

commentree

commentary; '1 a set of explanatory or critical notes on a text etc'.

2 'a descriptive spoken account (esp. on radio or television) of an event or a performance as it happens'.

Includes: sportscasters, newsreaders, reporters, gossip columnists, social commentators and others self-identifying as 'influencers.'

Additional Information: An overabundance of this species in one's make-up shows up in those inane people who always have something to say, dominate a discussion, have an opinion which is absolute and never listen to anyone else's point of view. They can usually be identified, even before they open their mouths, if you look at their ears. They are usually smaller than the average human ear. During my working life I came across many people obviously blessed with an overabundance of this tree gene. One male in particular stands out in my memory, so much so, I formed the opinion that the only reason evolution allowed his ears to remain intact was because they were needed solely for the purpose of supporting the arms of his glasses. Evolution has a wonderful way of gradually eliminating parts of the anatomy that are seldom used.

Nearest related type: elucidatrees.

complimentree

complimentary; 'of the nature of conveying or addressing a compliment: politely flattering'.

Nearest related type: congratulatrees.

condemnatree

condemnatory; 'censorious, critical, damning, reproving, reproachful, deprecatory, disapproving, unfavourable'.

Includes: fire-and-brimstone preachers, religious zealots, former hanging judges, prosecution lawyers, some mothers-in-law and those people who generally have a chip on their shoulder over just about anything.

Additional information: Some people just seem to have a strong trait here as part of their nature, irrespective of what vocation they have. For better or for worse, the mediums of X (formerly Twitter), Instagram and the like draw these types (trolls) out like blowflies around a fresh cow pat. To many, it would not be unfair to speculate that the characteristics of a combination of this species with a *bigatree* can be observed in an American President who vowed to 'Make America Great Again'. This is a good example of the power of our treevolutionary traits influencing human characteristics and behaviour

Nearest related types: derogatrees, commentrees.

congratulatree

congratulatory; 'conveying good wishes to someone in response
to an achievement or special occasion'.

Nearest related type: complimentrees.

conservatree

conservatory; 'a greenhouse for tender plants; a room esp. one
attached to and communicating with a house, designed for the growing
or displaying of plants'.

Includes: gardeners, landscapers, naturalists, nursery and *forestree*
workers, environmentalists, and in Australia, Greens political party
aspirants, perhaps.

Additional information: At the time of writing, a Google search of
the word 'conservatory' listed a total of 751,000 sites. I am certain that
many of these sites would have something to add to this work, but the
time needed to do each one the justice it deserves and an overwhelming
sense of just where to start, clearly is beyond me. The numbers above
are only surpassed by those sites listed for the word *'forestree'* (now see
if you can resist the temptation to jump ahead and check the number).
If you think about how many people would be involved with each of
these sites, one begins to appreciate just how many humans on planet
earth are so deeply connected to their ancestral roots. In the context
of this work, of all the English words relating to trees, *conservatree* has
to be the most appropriate word to support treevolution. With just
a small adjustment from its current English spelling, its meaning is
clear – 'conserve a tree'.

Nearest related type: forestrees.

contradictree

contradictory; 1 'expressing a denial or opposite statement'.

2 (of statements etc.) mutually opposed or inconsistent'.

Includes: predominantly politicians (especially evident when in
opposition); the general trait is negativity or pessimism.

Additional information: I recall reading once that, at any given time, somewhere in the world, there is a human holding up a placard declaring that this day is the end of the world for mankind. Sadly, for these poor souls, the soup of their ancestral mix has not been kind. Their predominant tree DNA would most likely be from *momentrees*.

Nearest related type: derogatrees.

countree

country; 1a 'the territory of a nation with its own government; a state. b a territory possessing its own language, people, culture, etc.'

Includes: accountants, auditors, treasurers, census takers, maths teachers. This key word has been discussed appropriately in previous chapters.

Nearest related types: budgetrees and depositrees.

dentistree

dentistry; 'the profession or practice of a dentist'.

Includes: dentists, orthodontists, oral hygienists, chewing gum and toothpaste manufacturers.

Additional information: It is possible that panel beaters working in the automotive crash repair business have elevated levels of this species. This tree type is discussed in the chapter The Theory of Treevolution and Medicine.

dietree

dietary; 'of or relating to a diet'.

Additional information: This is an interesting word and poses somewhat of a conundrum. The word itself literally reads as 'die-tree'. I suspect it does not represent a tree type as such but arose in retrospect to apply to trees that died as a result of poor nutrition, leading to the current day meaning and those related professions such as dieticians, nutritionists, naturopaths and so on.

Nearest related type: cemetrees.

derogatree

derogatory; 'involving disparagement or discredit; insulting, depreciatory (made a derogatory remark; derogatory to my position)'.

Includes: these trees are most likely to be close relatives with *contradictrees*, so the same vocational links would be similar, perhaps with the addition of food, film, travel and literary critics. General trait is negativity and/or pessimism.

Nearest related type: condemnatrees.

depositree

depository; 'a person to whom something is entrusted; a trustee'. a cache, store, storeroom, storehouse, warehouse, vault, safe, treasury, container, receptacle'.

Includes: hoarders and people who stockpile toilet paper during real or perceived civil instability are influenced by this gene.

Nearest related types: countrees, depositrees and monetrees.

desultree

desultory; '1 going constantly from one subject to another esp. in a half-hearted way 2 disconnected; unmethodical; superficial'.

Additional information: With descriptions like these, this may have possibly been the first human tree species that began experimentation with drugs! The taint of this species may be the reason for differences in the susceptibilities of people who are lured into taking drugs. What a find it would be if this link could lead to a suitable treatment.

Nearest related types: arbitrees and perfunctrees.

dignitree

dignitary; 'a person holding high rank or office, especially [in] government or religious organisations'.

Includes: the list of candidates descended from this lineage is as obvious as it is long. Bigwigs is an often-used, tree-related slang word to describe some important or powerful people. There is a probable link to the legal fraternity, evidenced today with the wearing of wigs during court proceedings. Generally used by those in lower echelons of society, the word usually means that their wig, or hair, which is the crown, is oversized in relation to the head, the inference being that they are overinflated with their own sense of importance. In Australia, there are a number of simpler words in general use to convey the same thing: boofhead, dickhead and wanker, for example.

dilatree

dilatory; 'given to or causing delay'. Slow, tardy, unhurried, sluggish, snail-like, lazy'.

Additional information: I am sure most people know someone for whom the above words are an apt behavioural description. After much reflection though, I feel that the word relates to one of several possibilities. Firstly, the name could have been used by our tree ancestors to differentiate the length of time a tree takes to die. Unlike *dietrees*, *dilatrees* take longer to pass away, that is to say, they die later. The second and more likely reason has to do with the communication between trees via the underground network of roots and fungi as discussed earlier. Perhaps they had to dial each other before they could be connected to a trunk call, and the term has been perpetuated, at least up until recent years before mobile phone systems took over. The third and most plausible reason (as if the previous two aren't plausible enough), has to be connected to the birth process of humans from trees. Although time passes at the same rate for us all, the same amount of time can seem an eternity or it can pass by in a flash, depending on the circumstances. For a pregnant woman about to give birth, the di-la-tree time before her child can be born must seem like an eternity, so one can only imagine how apt the description above would have been for a tree giving birth to a human. Another quandary for some budding young scientific researcher to unravel.

directree

directory; 'a book listing alphabetically or thematically a particular group of individuals'.

(e.g. telephone subscribers) or organisations with various details.' 'An alphabetical list of names and addresses of people in a city, town, building, etc.'

Includes: cartographers, surveyors, traffic cops, ushers, information/tourist centre offices, roadworks stop/go sign holders and generally all those people who have a penchant for telling others where to go! As a general observation, male humans have a higher percentage of this ancestral mix than women, certainly when it comes to directions in a 'map' sense, like finding the car in a carpark.

discriminatree

discriminatory; 'making a distinction, esp. unjustly and on the basis of race, colour, age, or sex.'

Additional information: All human nationalities have people (racists) who are tainted with the genetic trait of these trees. Hopefully one day, our scientists will be able to produce a vaccine that can eradicate this disease of the mind and heart, and John Lennon can rest in peace, knowing that the world has finally been made a better place.

Nearest related type: bigatrees.

disentree

dysentery; 'a disease with inflammation of the intestines, causing severe diarrhoea with blood.' Additional information: can be found in the chapter on Treevolution and Medicine.

documentree

documentary; '1 consisting of documents (*documentary evidence*). 2 providing a factual record or report.'

Includes: biographers, textbook writers, filmmakers, a small percentage of newspaper and magazine reporters. A classic example of a well-known identity who would have a strong lineage to these trees is Sir David Attenborough.

dormitree

dormitory; 'a sleeping room with several beds, esp. in a school or institution'.

Additional information: It is probable that there are no vocational outcomes from these trees, and they were so named either because timber was mostly used to make the beds in *dormitrees* or more likely, with reference to the similarities of a sleeping human to a dormant deciduous species of tree. A classic sign of those with above average *dormitree* DNA is easily observed in those people who have difficulty getting out of bed in the mornings, particularly in winter. This trait is exacerbated if, in addition to *dormitree* genes, their predominant species mix is from deciduous trees. I can certainly relate to this, as professed in my self-analysis at the end of this chapter. At this point, I think it is prudent to pass on some advice for parents of teenagers.

If you have just read the above, please do not jump to the conclusion that your teenager is cursed with a tree DNA profile with ninety plus per cent of this species. Just as humans experience changes in hormones throughout life, in most cases, your teenager will have other factors in their tree make-up that will exert a balancing effect within a few years.

elementree

elementary; '1a dealing with or arising from the simplest facts of a subject; rudimentary, introductory. b simple'.

Includes: scientists, pathologists, detectives such as Sherlock Holmes. *Elementrees* were most likely one of the first types of trees to evolve that were capable of communicating with humans. Their role would have been to teach basic knowledge or common sense to future generations. No doubt, Adam and Eve – or as I prefer, T1 and T2, as discussed in The Theory of Treevolution and Religion – were descendants of this species.

elucidatree

elucidatory; 'throw light on; explain'. explanatory, clarifying, illuminating, interpreting'.

Additional information: related to *commentrees*. All good teachers and communicators have this tree gene.

entree

entry; 'the act or an instance of going or coming in; liberty to go or come in, permission or right to enter; act of entering.'

Includes: militree guards, security guards, bodyguards, bouncers, doormen at hotels, ushers and ticket takers at sporting and event grounds. These trees are no doubt closely related to *sentrees*. It is probable that most dog species are related to these trees as they have a strong instinct to protect their master's property.

Additional information: To prevent any possible misunderstanding, I feel compelled to stress that entrees have nothing to do here with the introductory course on a restaurant menu. Although we know some primitive human cultures were cannibalistic, I have not been able to find a shred of evidence to suggest that our British tree ancestors were in any way linked to this practice! The origins of the word can be traced back to 16th century France. The word referred to the first course of a sumptuous, regal meal, brought to the table by a procession of liveried servants to the sound of trumpet fanfare. I only mention this to deter any suggestion that the French may have had people-eating ancestors, so I will leave it at that. The last thing I want to do is to strain relationships between *countrees*.

Nearest related types: sentrees, militrees and territrees.

explanatree

explanatory; 'serving or intended to serve to explain'. descriptive, illustrative, illuminative, elucidatory'.

Includes: teachers, storytellers, scriptwriters, marketing executives, conmen (there is a fine line between these last two).

Additional information: It is likely that this species is interrelated with *planetrees* and *interplanetrees*. Perhaps they were the early custodians of tree knowledge and wisdom. Could they have held secrets of their relations above that allude to them coming from another planet? Another *mystree* for the scientific community to solve. Then again, it is possible that the 'ex' merely refers to *planetrees* that were deceased or perhaps outed as *purgatrees* for one reason or another.

Nearest related types: elucidatrees, commentrees and documentrees.

expositree

expository; 'explanatory, descriptive, describing, elucidatree, explicatree, interpretive'.

Additional information: Related to explanatrees and thereby to *planetrees* and *interplanetrees*. This species could have given rise to the earliest spies, exposing undesirable trees such as *adultrees* perhaps. Then again, their species name could also suggest that they were related to *adultrees* or *rudimentrees* if they had always been exposing themselves in whatever constituted inappropriate tree behaviour! It is possible that the behavioural consequences of high levels of this species DNA in humans' manifests in those who frequent nudist beaches, or some who become exhibitionists, usually triggered by excessive levels of alcohol, who somehow think that streaking naked on a packed sporting ground is a good idea.

Nearest related types: explanatrees, commentrees and elucidatrees.

exploratree

exploratory; '1 (of discussion etc.) preliminary, serving to establish procedure etc. 2 of or concerning exploration or investigation (exploratory surgery).'

Additional information: All of the great explorers the world has ever known must have descended from *exploratrees*. In truth, most humans have at least some of this type in their genetic make-up (the possible exception being *sedentrees*). Our tree ancestors would have known that their human forms would need to confront very different circumstances to theirs. Somehow, whether by design or just good luck, they managed to pass down some genetic instinct that pushed their mobile offspring to explore and learn quickly in their new surroundings. Without this natural urge, it is quite probable humans would never have survived, or if they did, they would have remained relatively primitive creatures. When we think of Australian explorers, most people think of early pioneers, such as Birk and Wills, Charles Sturt, Hubert Wilkins and Douglas Mawson. Birch trees symbolise new beginnings, as they take root in landscapes where no other tree has been able to grow. They are traditionally thought of as being pioneers.

flattree

flattery; 1 'exaggerated or insincere praise, 2 the act or an instance of flattering.'

Additional information: Perhaps related to *battrees* that have no energy, or trees that have been blown over!

Nearest related types: probably congratulatrees and complimentrees, but links to approbatrees and cemetrees cannot be ruled out.

forestree

forestry; '1 the science or management of forests 2 wooded country; forests; the practice of planting and taking care of trees.'

Includes: foresters, park rangers, lumberjacks, woodsmen, loggers and tree fellers (for anyone of Irish descent who may read this, 'tree fellers' is a similar occupation to lumberjacks and does not mean three individual persons).

Additional information: Further to my previous tease in the definition for *conservatree*, the number of Google hits for *forestree* was 751,000, just enough to spend a few lifetimes poring through. Forrest ranks as the 292nd most common surname in England, with over 30,000 people sharing this surname and the highest concentration of Forrests is in Norfolk (4,824 people). The name was introduced by the Normans who invaded England around 1056 AD and referred to a Royal Forest, which presumably means a stand of trees owned by a King rather than a King whose name was Forrest.

gallantree

gallantry; '1 bravery, dashing, courage 2 courtliness; devotion to women 3 a polite act or speech.'

Includes: Englishmen of noble breeding epitomised *gallantrees*, at least in years past. I bemoan the fact that the modern world seems to have lost a great number of this types' true descendants, largely through the sanitising of character and language through the unfortunate growth of the political correctness movement. We are all the poorer for it. No doubt the suffragettes epitomised trees with this gene.

Nearest related type: gentrees.

gantree

gantry; 'an overhead structure with a platform supporting a travelling crane, or railway or road signals.'

Includes: bridge builders, roofing contractors, etc.

Additional information: The great churches of Europe with their high arches and domes would have been erected by descendants of these trees. Generally, anyone who loves climbing trees or has a desire to build a tree house would have a percentage of their genetic make-up from this lesser-known species. The Sydney Harbour Bridge is a good example of an Australian *gantree* bridge. Perhaps those who built it were from *gantree* lineage, the most notable being Paul Hogan of Crocodile Dundee fame, who worked on this bridge for many years in his youth. A search reveals only four people in England having this surname (Gantry), and 24 in the USA. This imbalance shows that the

Americans probably enticed *gantrees* to America during the eighteenth century to help with bridge building. Sadly, they appear to be a highly endangered species.

Nearest related type: carpentrees.

gentree

gentry; 'the class of people next below the nobility in position and birth.'

Additional information: Perhaps I have been influenced by the various films and television series such as Downton Abbey and Judge John Deed, and books on English schools (like Tom Brown's School Days) but I find it difficult to believe that any other *countree* in the world could match the English Aristocracy for their association, involvement and fervour with the definition and descriptions of gentry above. Surely, *gentrees* could only evolve from English descent and this word helps to confirm my belief that only the English language provides the links to our evolution from trees.

Nearest related type: gallantrees. On the downside, they could also be related to bigatrees.

geometree

geometry; 'the branch of mathematics concerned with the properties and relations of points, lines, surfaces and solids.'

Includes: maths teachers, astronomers, architects, draughters (to be politically correct), mariners, landscapers.

Nearest related types: countrees and observatrees.

hereditree

hereditary; '1 of disease, instinct etc., able to be passed down from one generation to another. 2a descending by inheritance.'

Additional information: In the context of this book, this word is one of the key links in the theory of treevolution and so is deserving of more in-depth analysis. Unlike other tree words that we can readily relate to either vocations or distinct human characteristics, *hereditree* seems to be a term that encompasses all trees, so it must be significant, but in what way? Tree species can be identified in so many ways: leaf shape, height, width, bark nature, trunk colour, evergreen or deciduous, life expectancy, softwood or hardwood, and so on.

If we look back through *histree* to the earliest records for insight as to how, when and why the word evolved, we find it first recorded in 1530. It comes from the Latin *hereditatum*, meaning 'condition of being an heir'. So, we look to the meaning of heir and come to 'a person legally entitled to the property or rank of another on that person's death.' Interesting and obvious as this is, it has little to do with the genetic aspect of the word *hereditree*. Of all the various dictionary definitions that use different words to say the same thing, one gave me a clue as to its true ancestral origins: 'The term hereditary is applied to diseases and characteristics such as the tendency toward baldness that passes from parents to children.' Suddenly, it all made sense. It was a lightbulb moment, and I had an FBO (flash of the bleeding obvious). The 'here' in the word is referring to the hair on a human's head. It literally means hair-of-the-tree! At the top of a tree is the crown, the uppermost part of a forest tree that gets the most sunlight, which is essential for the tree's survival. To this day, even though it is rapidly becoming far less common than I recall in my earlier years, the term 'his or her crowning glory' is used to describe one's head of hair. Obviously, when the first human trees began evolving hundreds of thousands of years ago, the leaves or bark that gradually developed into hair at the top of the head would have been vital for survival, both from a pure physical requirement and also as a desirability trait to facilitate procreation. Today, we have evolved to the point where we no longer need head hair for survival, but does that mean we take our hair for granted? I suggest this key genetic link is the driving force behind many humans' almost-obsessive quests to have a good head of hair. The industries that have evolved around supplying hair products, cutting and styling services and the money that is spent worldwide is surely out of proportion to any actual benefit to our health in general, or indeed, our survival. Again, this an example of just how powerful our ancestral roots can be.

Before I move on, if you are reading this and are concerned about your hair, or more specifically, your lack of hair (particularly if you are male), I offer this advice. From an external observation viewpoint, trees can be separated pretty much into one of two categories – evergreen or deciduous. Depending on your ancestral and *hereditree* mixes over the centuries you will have the dominant characteristics of either one of these two types. We all know people who still have a good crown well into their later years of life, irrespective of their lifestyles. Correspondingly, we all know people who have lost their hair much earlier in life, irrespective of their lifestyles. Our often-desperate desire to return our forest crown to its former glory paves the way for unscrupulous enterprises to make fortunes with potions and procedures promising to restore your balding pate back to its former glory. My advice is this: don't waste your time and money. The reality is, no potion or outlandish advice – such as standing on your head for hours to get blood flow to your dormant hair follicles – will make one iota of difference to tens of thousands of years of genetic programming. If your genetic mix is predominantly from deciduous trees, you will lose your hair and short of going back a few hundred thousand years in a time machine and interfering in a match up with your ancestors and getting them to mate with evergreen species, there is nothing you can do about it. Having stated that, there may be an opportunity for an enterprising scientific based company to make products that could change this.

Earlier in my introduction, I expressed my thoughts and feelings around discovering the links between trees and humans and that it needed someone with the ability to see things from an outward overview. With that in mind, consider the following: if I am correct with my assumption that our hair health is directly related to our mix of deciduous and evergreen heritage and we could find a significant difference in the internal functions between them, we might be able to pinpoint the mechanisms by which the evergreens hold on to their foliage. One significant difference between trees is that while all trees contain sap, only those belonging to the Pinaceae family, namely coniferous trees like pine, cedar and Douglas fir, have both sap and resin. Sap is waterier than resin, which is thick and sticky. The function of sap to transport vital mineral nutrients and sugars to all parts of the tree is well understood, but scientists are still divided as to whether tree resin is a waste product or a means of protection against infection or insect attack. Perhaps this resin also plays a role in an evergreen tree's ability to hold onto its foliage. If someone isolated the relevant gene, patented it, and used it in a tablet or drink, a lot of men and women would be very happy, not to mention the company that held the patent.

While on this subject, in the chapter The Most Royal Trees, I wrote that there is a special link between treevolution and the British Royal Family. As odd as this sounds, it has to do with their hair. It would be a fair assumption to state that members of the Royal Family would have the means to unearth a treatment for baldness if one was available? So, no guesses for working out which of the two types of genetic tree predominance has bestowed itself on Princes William and Harry, who can no longer hide their deciduous tree ancestry. William and Harry's father, King Charles on the other hand, despite being older, still had a good 'crown' up into his 60s – obviously gifted from a stronger mix of evergreen DNA. Prince William and Harry's receding hairlines would have been affected through the infusion of deciduous tree genes from their mother, who did not have the royal evergreen tree genes.

hortatree

hortatory; 'tending or serving to exhort'. Urging to some course of conduct or action; encouraging; inciting.

Includes: I cannot think of any current day careers that would have developed from this species. However, a liberal sprinkling of this tree in one's ancestral mix could result in urges to become a protester, dissenter, rebel, union leader, cheerleader or just a downright troublemaker! Despots and dictators have a higher percentage of this DNA than normal (think Adolf Hitler). On an everyday level, a strong link with this species can sometimes be seen in parents at children's sports events. They are the ones who go beyond the normal bounds of cheering from the sidelines, often strutting along the perimeter of play bellowing instructions to their poor offspring who are being exhorted to be the superstar their parent never was. On the positive, I suspect that some *hortatree* heritage could be beneficial if it is matched with a higher proportion of *oratree* DNA. All great leaders have probably had such a blend, although sadly, there seems to be fewer of them in today's world probably due to over-deforestation of the forests that contained trees with this specific characteristic.

HISTREE

histree

history; '1a continuous, usu. chronological record of important or public events. 2a the study of past events, esp. human affairs.' the branch of knowledge dealing with past events';

Includes: historians, archaeologists, librarians; generally, those people who have a fascination with web sites like ancestree.com. and television programs like the *histree* channel on Foxtel.

Additional information: Related to *documentrees*, people with a genetic mix of these trees may tend to live in the past. This work hinges on the *histree* of words etched into the English language, so I find the timing of my work oddly ironic in that one of the great challenges facing *histree* is the English language itself. There is an evolving group of humans who, for whatever reason, seem hell-bent on trying to either emasculate men or transmogrify the male and female human species into one sex. While the evolutionary prospect of eventually being able to mate with oneself to continue the human species may be an upside, I, for one, hope that the powerful forces we have inherited from our tree ancestors prevents this from happening.

Let me elaborate. Barely a week goes by where we do not see or hear of an article in the media where one or more of these self-appointed politically correct persons ventures forth with the next list of words in the English language that they deem to be sexist and demeaning. Essentially, it appears to me that these people want to change any word with any reference to the male species so that it appears as non-gender specific. One of the first casualties I recall was the change of the word 'manhole cover' to 'personal inspection plate' or 'utility hole'. If women are now involved in work that requires them to pull up these round metal plates that proliferate our streets (oh, why can't they site them in the middle of the road or in between the white lines so we can all enjoy a smoother ride) then fair enough. By all means, change the word 'mannequin' to 'womanequin', 'feminequin' or 'bodyquin' or whatever. If the word 'manacles' (handcuffs, shackles, chains, irons, fetters, restraints, bonds) is deemed sexist, I for one have no objection to it being changed to 'femnacles', or 'womnacles', or having both variations, to be applied appropriately based on the gender of the person needing to be manacled. Let's face it, when was the last time you heard your average Aussie bloke getting upset about sexist or *derogatree* wording? I am sure that if we called animal excretia 'feminure' or 'womanure' there would be all hell to pay, but most men are not worried in the slightest that we are directly implicated in the word 'manure' – we just don't give a four-letter word starting with the letter 's'.

This move for political correctness at the expense of what most good people would deem to be common sense is a worldwide dilemma (at least in western *countrees*) as the following examples illustrate. A school in Seattle renamed Easter eggs 'spring spheres' to avoid causing offence to people who did not celebrate Easter. A UK council banned the term 'brainstorming' and replaced it with 'thought showers', as local lawmakers thought the term may offend epileptics. A UK recruiter had her job advertisement for 'reliable and hardworking' people rejected by the job centre on the grounds that it could be offensive to unreliable and lazy people! Really?!! Closer to home, in 2007, in Sydney, all Santa Clauses were banned from saying 'Ho Ho Ho'. Their employer, the recruitment firm Westaff, allegedly told all trainees that 'Ho Ho Ho' could frighten children and be *derogatree* to some women – because 'Ho' was considered too close to the American slang term for prostitute! Really? Has anyone done a count of just how many American sex workers are in Australia and asked them if they were offended? If they did find a few, being American, they probably would have said it was good for advertising, so leave the word in!

On a slightly more positive, if not cynical note, I seriously doubt the Chinese people will be removing all reference to Ho Chi Minh City any time soon. I only mention this because Australia will probably be owned by the Chinese within the next fifty years when English will be relegated to a secondary language, at best, and the 'need' for any sanitising of the English language will no longer be under our control. Fair dinkum, the world is going mad when things get to this level of lunacy.

Once the 'man' has been taken out from every word it will only be a matter of time before the 'his' in *histree* will be next on the hitlist. Get used to your kids studying 'femtory', or perhaps 'womtory' at school. Perhaps it may be appropriate to retain the word *histree* when it comes to writing about the past events for or by males and introduce *herstree* for females, with *theirstree* for all other human classifications! I say this because the word history, with the addition of only one letter and a space becomes - his story. Given that the vast majority of *histree* has been written by men, I feel this wording is no coincidence, and it is about time women are given the opportunity to record their versions of past events in equal measure.

Even a simple trip to the local vegetable shop is going to require a change in thinking – prepare yourself in future to ask for a 'femgo' instead of a mango. Perhaps though, they may leave the humble mango until the very last, after every other word containing any reference to man or his has been erased. Rubbing salt into the wounds of men the world over, I feel sure the PC crowd may find some perverse pleasure in leaving the word 'mango' intact before inflicting the final insult by adding the two letters that validate their *victree*, by calling it a mangone!

I dare say these word police will be selective about leaving a few words unchanged. Apart from manacles and manure, they will not make a big fuss over changing a smelly mosquito infected swamp from a 'mangrove' to a 'femgrove' and I am equally sure that the word maniac will endure, along with men doing menial tasks!

On a more serious note, unless there is a confirmed link with only males of the human species, I think the medical name for the illness meningitis is in need of a more gender-neutral name. For similar reasons the name for that rare but potentially devastating disease, meningococcal, also needs gender-balancing, but should only be retained if there is a need for a term to describe the activity of two or more adult males in a boat, who are opening crustaceans to bait their hooks before trying to catch fish.

I realise that, by now, it may appear as though I have gone off the rails a bit with all this. However, it is important to realise that the whole essence of this book is based on those threads of the English language that still remain to enable us to trace our heritage back to where we all began – trees. At the rate words are being changed and disbanded, within a short span of *histree*, we may lose all perspective with our past. Perhaps the words of Mark Twain best sum up this whole conundrum: 'Sometimes I wonder whether the world is run by smart people who are putting us on, or by imbeciles who really mean it.' Sadly, I suspect it may be the latter.

Now, I must move on with renewed haste with this work, so that I can at least forward a **man**uscript to potential publishers.

THE I TO Z OF TREE WORDS

idolatree

idolatry; '1 the worship of idols. 2 great adulation, reverence or devotion'.

Additional information: The genetic influence of this type afflicts people in varying degrees of intensity, ranging from the usually innocuous teenage adulation of boy pop bands to the more dangerous end of the spectrum where people get coerced into joining cults, many of which are ruled by a charismatic male psychopath. The worst level is where people come to believe that joining a terrorist group like ISIL is somehow a great way to leave a positive mark on society. Personally, if *idolatrees* still existed as tree types and could be identified, I, for one, would be in favour of severely curtailing their influence.

industree

industry; '1 a branch of trade or manufacture; 2 concerted or copious activity. 3 diligence 4 habitual employment in useful work.'

Additional information: In contrast to *idolatrees*, the qualities of *industrees* on an individual level (through the word industrious) are most desirable for humans to thrive. These qualities include being hardworking, diligent, assiduous, conscientious, steady, painstaking, persistent, unflagging, tireless, indefatigable and studious. It should be no surprise to anyone that the industrial revolution started in Britain. An enterprising man by the name of Sir Richard Arkwright developed the spinning machine, which marked a shift from the cottage *industree* to powered, special purpose machinery and hence *factrees* (factories) and mass production. This in turn led to more jobs for the masses. A healthy mix of this species in your genetic mix goes a long way to making your life a success in whatever vocation you choose. The potentially tragic irony is that these are the same qualities that have led to many of the world's problems, the key ones being pollution and the move of humans away from the laws of nature. The paradox is that these are the very issues our tree ancestors are trying to warn us about through the messages left in the English language.

inflammatrees

inflammatory; '1 tending to cause anger etc. 2 of or tending to inflammation of the body.'

Additional information: The genetic influences of this type can be noticed in people whose emotions overrule the logical parts of their brains. Nowhere is this more evidenced than in two-year-old humans who have not yet developed any control over these ancestral tree influences – hence the term 'the terrible twos' and 'temper tantrums.' *Inflammatree* behaviour is often on display in sport, particularly professional sport, when elevated stress levels allow this gene to cause dramatic behavioural changes, frequently leading to spectacular meltdowns. Tennis is one sport that readily comes to mind – and when they let fly, they really make (or most likely break) a racket (sadly, the effect of this species is becoming evident in the top levels of Australian tennis)! They can also be found in the realms of social media forums, such as X (formerly known as Twitter). Online bullies would most certainly have *inflammatree* DNA in them. Physical *inflammatree* behaviour manifests in people who become arsonists and at the extreme level there have been examples of people who have inexplicably self-combusted! There are some 200 recorded occurrences of this phenomenon, dating back as far as 1470, with many varied theories put forward as to how this could happen. These people no doubt had high levels of *inflammatree* tree DNA in their genes. Unfortunately, excessive amounts of this gene can lead to people becoming terrorist suicide bombers (they would probably have a higher-than-average amount of *momentree* genetic make-up as well). Hopefully, if these trees still exist and can be identified, vaccines might be developed to prevent, or severely curtail, this form of extremism, and we may be able to formulate medicines to help people suffering from *inflammatree* conditions, such as rheumatoid arthritis. Fortunately, not all *inflammatree* influences are bad. Without some level of this species in our genetic mix, we probably wouldn't have those people who delight the masses with wonderful pyrotechnic fireworks displays at major public events, like New Year's Eve. The comic superhero 'The Torch' is also founded on the basis of this tree type.

anti-inflammatrees

Additional information: This genus is an example of how tree evolution evolved to negate the undesirable effects of a particular species. The security of forests with a few *inflammatrees* amongst them will always be under constant threat. It would only need one or two of these to self-combust and the whole forest could be lost. Anti-*inflammatrees* evolved to counteract the influence of *inflammatrees*. Without some influence from this species, where would we get our dedicated firefighters?

interplanetree

interplanetary; '1 between planets. 2 relating to travel between planets.'

Additional information: Could it be possible that this species came from another world and developed into the original trees from which all others on Earth evolved? This is a fascinating concept and beyond the scope of this work. However, if one day it could be confirmed, how wonderfully ironic would it be to realize we have spent so much time and effort investigating whether there is life on other planets, only to discover that we ourselves are the descendants of life from another world? Perhaps the first and subsequent humans to have walked on the moon have the DNA of this species in their genetic make-up.

inventree

inventory; '1 a complete list of goods in stock, house contents etc., a complete listing of work, goods, etc.'

Includes: auditors, accountants, bookkeepers, actuaries, and quantity surveyors. No doubt, *inventrees* and *industrees* are closely related, the former presumably evolving before the latter.

Additional information: I would have thought, though, that the name would imply that descendants of this tree would most likely be inventors. Sir Richard Arkwright was certainly one, as well as having strong *industree* links.

Nearest related type: possibly budgetrees.

laboratree

laboratory; 'a room or building fitted for scientific experiments, research, teaching, or the manufacture of drugs and chemicals.'

Includes: Scientists, chemists, coroners, lab technicians, chemical manufacturers, members of an Australian political party perhaps, and as alluded to below, midwives.

Additional information: As discussed in the chapter The Theory of Treevolution and the First Australians, in Australia, there are sites where hollowed out trees are referred to as 'birthing trees' by Aboriginal people. With a culture that goes back some 60,000 years, this must raise the possibility that trees in Europe and other parts of the world were also utilized in this way, supporting the likelihood that *laboratrees* derived from a generic term used to define all pregnant female trees. The term for a woman giving birth as 'being in labour' may have less to do with the physical act of giving birth, but more so to the fact that she is giving birth under the protection of one of these spiritual trees.

laudatree

laudatory; 'expressing praise, complimentary congratulatory, extolling, adulatory, commendatory, approbatory, flattery, celebratory, eulogizing'.

Includes: celebrants typically, and generally all political aspirants, as well as sycophants and brown nosers.

Nearest related types: complimentrees, congratulatrees, adulatrees, commendatrees, approbatrees, flattrees and celebratrees.

lavatree

lavatory; 'a receptacle into which a person can urinate or defecate, usu. with a flush mechanism as a means of disposing of the products.'water closet, public convenience, cloakroom, powder room, urinal, privy, latrine'.

Additional information: This is one of the most interesting tree types, particularly as most people have a frequent and personal daily affinity for its namesake, the modern-day lavatory. It is also one of the most mysterious trees as its origins are unclear, just as the waters of its current day namesake are often unclear! There are several theories as to its origins. One train of thought links the name with ancient times in Italy, when the Romans were into building aqueducts, sewers and the like. At that time, there were also active volcanoes in the area, and the Romans noticed that some trees in the paths of the molten flows, although killed, remained upright, albeit covered by the cooling molten rock they named lava, hence the name lava-tree. The link between this theory and the modern-day convenience we use today is most likely due to the similarity in the nature of cooled lava and modern ceramics. This reasoning is accorded more credence from the definition of the word lava – 'hot molten or semi fluid rock erupted from a volcano or fissure'. I am sure most of us can relate to that on a very personal level at one time or another during our lives! Another suggestion is that the name has its origins much earlier in *histree*, during the times of the Egyptian pharaohs and in particular, King Tutankhamon, the boy king. Whether King Tut had an early form of the modern toilet or not is unclear, but in my early childhood I remember my parents making reference to going to the 'tut' or 'tuttie', meaning the toilet – which is yet another word and its *histree* destined for extinction. The only linking reference I could find suggests the word came from the Punjab region of India and is still widely understood throughout India today. Pronounced 'tut-tee', it is a slang word for human excrement. It is likely that this word and its meaning became known here from the English occupation of India, just as it would have travelled and prevailed all that time from Egypt to India. Hopefully, for the sake of King Tut's historical record, the word derived as a result of his pioneering of the squatus porcelaina ceramica that we are so dependent on today, and not as a result of any really bad thoughts his people had of him!

Fascinating though these two thoughts on the origins of *lavatrees* may be, the concern I had was that neither of them has a link to our tree ancestors. This could raise serious questions as to the validity of the whole point of this work. It was only when I was writing the chapter on treevolution and sex that the answer became apparent. *Lavatrees* came from lover-trees. They are doubtless intertwined with *adultrees, amatrees, sultrees* and the odd *purgatree* or two, but consider how different the world would be without their influence. From the myriad of film stars of both sexes whose revolving door scandals provide literary fodder for the masses and learning examples for our children of what not to do to be successful in relationships, to that tall, long-haired, handsome chap who graced the television screens of Australia a few years ago, flogging some margarine spread with the words, 'I can't believe it's not budder,' the world would be a much duller place without the descendants of this species. The downside is that many trees are felled to provide the paper needed to fuel their goings-on through the print media.

lottree

lottery; '1 a means of raising money by selling numbered tickets and giving prizes to the holders of numbers drawn at random; 2 an enterprise, process etc., whose success is governed by chance. (life is a lottery).'

Additional information: the word most likely relates to the word lot, meaning 'a large number or amount' of trees. In past times, when forests dominated the landscape and human populations were much smaller than today, the chances of getting found in a lot of trees diminished the bigger the lot became. No guesses needed here to see why the word is in use today. We all know the odds in these government-sanctioned lot-of-trees. Still, the influence of this species is widespread and very powerful, so much so that in far too many cases, humans fall under their spell and succumb to the addictions of gambling, much to their own detriment and that of those close to them.

Nearest related types: countrees and sentrees – somebody has to count and guard the money!

mandatree

mandatory; '1 of or conveying a demand. 2 compulsory.'

Includes: dictators, unionists, typically.

Additional information: as with the inference above to *laboratrees* being female gender-specific, it is likewise possible that the name *mandatree* came about from a generic term used to define male trees, namely man-da-tree. This species has been discussed in the previous chapter, Treevolution and The Origins of Armed Forces.

mastree

mastery; '1 dominion, sway. 2 masterly skill. 3 (often foll. by of) comprehensive knowledge, or use of a subject or instrument.'

Additional information: This word is most likely a generic term referring to any species of tree that had very straight, durable timber used to make masts on a boat or ship. As such, it is likely to have evolved within the last 400 years and may not be representative of any ancient human ancestor. Certainly, the current words used to define *mastree* are consistent with what would be needed to climb one of these masts, particularly the grasp and grip aspects. It could also be a word used to identify any tree of a species that has a mast year, which is a year yielding larger amounts of seeds or nuts than most other years.

migratree

migratory; '1 (of people) moving from one place of abode to another, esp. in a different country. 2 (of an animal. esp. a bird or fish) changing its area of habitation with the seasons.'

Additional information: These trees were no doubt closely related to *exploratrees* and are no doubt the true pioneers in our tree ancestors' quest to cover the earth. Their DNA is more observable in the *migratree* habits of many species of animals, especially birds, whose epic journeys to feeding and breeding grounds each year are remarkable. About one in five bird species are *migratree*. Modern civilisation over the past 200 years has all but curtailed the *migratree* characteristics of many human cultures, such as the American Indians and the Australian Aboriginals, who were nomadic before European settlement.

Nearest related type: exploratrees.

militree

military; 'of, or relating to, or characteristic of soldiers or armed forces, as distinct from civilians and the police.'

Additional information: more detail on *militrees* and their associated species is discussed in the chapter Treevolution and the Origins of Armed Forces.

Nearest related species: sentrees. Associated with countrees and parliamentrees.

minatree

minatory; 'threatening, menacing.'

Includes: Debt collectors, bikie gang members, trade union officials and bullies in general. Some breeds of dogs used primarily as guard dogs have high levels of this species in their genetic make-up.

Nearest related types: bigatrees and predatrees.

ministree

ministry; '1 a government department headed by a minister. 2 the vocation or profession of a religious minister *(called to the ministry)* 3 the office of a religious minister, priest, etc.'

Includes: pastors, rectors, bishops, cardinals, priests, chaplains, padres – even the odd Pope.

Nearest related types: monastrees, rectrees and vestrees.

momentree

momentary; '1 lasting only a moment. 2 short-lived, transitory.'

Additional information: Obviously, there can be no long-lasting vocational opportunities for those afflicted with this genetic timebomb. The many books titled The Darwin Awards, by Wendy Northcutt, contain countless examples of humans (mainly males) removing themselves from the human gene pool though various acts of idiotic stupidity. The numerous authenticated examples in these books elicit pathos and humour and an overall feeling of, 'just how did these people live as long as they did?' A recent example (not in the above books, yet) comes to mind of the terrorist who made and sent a letter bomb to his intended target but had the parcel returned due to insufficient postage! Thinking it was a parcel to him, he unfortunately opened it but did not have time to at least appreciate that he had done a competent job of making the device. Now that is karma. One can only wonder what type of trees *momentrees* looked like, but my guess is that they didn't live long enough to be very tall.

Nearest related types: there are few, if any, near tree relatives to this tree type other than possibly transitrees and arbitrees.

monastree

monastery; 'the residence of a religious community, esp. of monks living in seclusion.'

Includes: monks, nuns, priests, gospel singers perhaps.

Nearest related types: ministrees, vestrees and rectrees.

monetree

monetary; '1 of the currency in use. 2 of or consisting of money.'

Includes: financial advisors, bankers, treasurers, accountants, actuaries, bank robbers. This tree type is probably the one that is likely to grab the interest of most people. We all need and want money, so it is prudent that we look at the influences of this tree on our lives in more detail. Firstly, we need to look at where the name came from. In historical terms, it is probable that the name is relatively recent and has no ancestral basis at all, instead being derived from the results of human enterprises involved with the trading of tree produce and products – everything from timber and wooden items through to fruits, nuts, oils, resins, spices and the like. On the other hand, the number of activities involving money that show the worst sides of human behaviour suggests that a far deeper force is operating within many of us. Thieves, robbers, pirates, embezzlers, loan sharks, scammers, pickpockets, money-launderers, and some lawyers and politicians coexist around financial enterprises like Australian blowflies around a cow pat. Fortunately, most 'normal' people operate their financial lives without resorting to these extremes. Regrettably, I have not been able to unearth any evidence to give hope that there is, or ever was, a money tree. The old idiom, 'money doesn't grow on trees' still holds true. Our recent ancestors were much more reliant on trees than we are today, and a lot of money would have changed hands over the years due to the influence of trees. It is possible that the often-used term 'money doesn't grow on trees' originated during times past, when what was produced and sold or traded from tree produce was as good as having money. Times change, and though trees and their bounty are still important parts of our lives, the more recent growth in the use of metals and plastics has reduced our reliance on them. So, in effect, in the past, it was like money grew from trees. Perhaps the correct expression should be 'money doesn't come from trees like it used to'!

In Australian politics, there is a fundamental historical difference in *monetree* dealings between the two major parties. The Liberal party, contrary to what the word 'liberal' means, are more responsible overall in handling the fiscal affairs of the country. Conversely, the Labor Party has a penchant for spending up big, often on batty projects that are at odds against what we in Australia call 'the pub test' (the law of bloody common sense). The political cycle between the two, while it may vary in the length of time, is almost hardwired into the minds of the electorate as illustrated by the following: Labor is in power until enough people come to the realisation that they are sending the *countree* broke, so they get booted out for the Liberals, who spend the next cycle trying to pay back the huge debt left by Labor's excessive spending. Usually, just about the time the Liberals have balanced the budget, people start groaning that they aren't spending enough on all sorts of issues, so they vote the Liberals out and reinstate Labor – and so the cycle starts again. The point here is that, overall, the Liberal Party must have more representatives descended from the more prudent tree types than their Labor counterparts (or put another way, the Liberals have slightly less numbers than Labor of those who could be considered to fit into the shadier tree type categories). I wish to state here that I am in no way trying to make a political statement. I am just outlining some historical facts to support my hypothesis. If one wishes to validate the above, knock yourself out digging through the records to find the last time a Labor Government reduced the national debt during their term in office.

Nearest related types: budgetrees and countrees.

mystree

mystery; '1 a secret, hidden or inexplicable matter (the reason remains a mystery). 2 secrecy or obscurity (wrapped in mystery).'

Includes: detectives, crime novelists, spies, cryptic crossword clue exponents. Most women have varying degrees of genetic inheritance from this species, at least from a man's perspective.

Nearest related types: amatrees, sultrees, perfunctrees and adultrees.

observatree

observatory; 'a room or building equipped for the observation of natural, esp. astronomical, or meteorological phenomena.'

Includes: astronomers and stargazers, scientists, spies, detectives, personal bodyguards, childminders, spectators

Additional information: Generally, anyone who can watch a sunset without getting bored, anyone who can stay focussed on a five-day game of test cricket without losing their sanity and anyone who can work out the murderer in episodes of TV series like *Poirot*, *Midsummer Murders* or the *Murdoch Mysteries*. One can easily see how these trees would have evolved. Our tree ancestors could not move and as far as I am aware, they did not sleep (except for the cooler-climate deciduous types in winter) so they would have had plenty of time to observe the heavens most nights. It is probable that these trees began as carers for smaller trees, eventually branching out into sub-species leading to their human descendants becoming involved in any one of the vocations listed above.

Nearest related types: planetrees, interplanetrees.

obligatree

obligatory; '1 legally or morally binding. 2 compulsory and not merely permissive. 3 constituting an obligation.'

Additional information: The influence of this tree can be observed in those people who are sticklers for adhering to the rules or the law. It's their way or the highway with virtually no room to negotiate. This genetic trait is in most humans and is essential, as without it, rules for a civilised society would not be followed and chaos and anarchy would ensue. All tyrants, despots and dictators have extreme levels of this gene. Military personnel have above average levels, while parking meter inspectors have slightly less, but more than the average. One of the worst humans you can encounter is one with a genetic mix of *obligatree, minatree* and *mandatree* DNA, resulting in a menacing, threatening, baleful, intimidating bully who has been sacked from their job as a debt collector and is now most likely a member of a dubious bikie gang. Adolf Hitler is undoubtedly a suitable example of a bad outcome of this triple combination.

Nearest related types: minatrees, mandatrees, and statutrees.

optometree

optometry; 'the measurement of the refractive power and other properties of the eyes and the prescription of corrective lenses; the occupation of an ophthalmic optician.'

Includes: optometrists, eyewear manufacturers, telescope makers, eye-laser technicians. This species is discussed in the chapter on The Theory of Treevolution and Medicine.

Nearest related type: observatrees.

oratrees

oratory; '1 the art or practice of formal speaking., esp. in public. 2 exaggerated, eloquent, or highly coloured language.'

Includes: public speakers, celebrants, politicians, stage actors, poets and possibly stand-up comedians.

Additional information: Oratrees are the most recent ancestors evolved from *laudatrees, explanatrees, elucidatrees, hortatrees* and *commentrees.* Sadly, this species seems to be in rapid decline, due largely to the increased scrutiny brought on by the proliferation of media communications and the political correctness element of society.

Nearest related types: dignitrees, laudatrees, explanatrees, elucidatrees, hortatrees and commentrees.

palmistree

palmistry; (also known as chiromancy); 'a method of divination by examination of the lines and swellings of the hand. The parts of the hand are held to correspond to various parts of the body, traits of personality, and to the celestial bodies.'

Additional information: I have never been tempted to have such a 'reading' done, having dismissed it as a con or a way of making money by preying on the weakness of peoples' minds. So, I find it somewhat ironic that this tree type may yet prove to be a key link between modern humans and our tree ancestors, thereby giving further credence to my theory. What initially piqued my interest in this word was a curiosity to see if there was some connection between an unbranched evergreen tree of tropical regions and that inside part of the human hand from the wrist to the base of the fingers, both of which are called a palm. From a purely physiological aspect, the lines on our palms are crease lines (palmar flexion creases) that allow us to scrunch our hand into a fist or other shape without excessive stretching of the skin. I can certainly attest to that, but on looking intently at my palms for probably the first time in my life, I could see many other lines of varying length and depth that did not appear to be necessary for palmar flexion. It's probably just the result of over seventy years of use, but my palm-line profiles look more like the striation marks made by rocks and boulders as they scrape across the landscape under the pressure of glaciers. They certainly do not look legible enough for anyone to predict future outcomes or divulge anything from my past, aside from the lines that were made when I flew over the handlebars of my bike and used my palms as brakes on the bitumen, when the chisel slipped, and at the site of my biggest splinter. My hands have been well used, and I am blessed I still have them both functioning.

Having tried to educate myself at a basic level with *palmistree* for the purposes of this book, the key points I have taken follow here. Firstly, the practice dates back thousands of years and is rooted in ancient scriptures of various religions. Secondly, interpreting character by the lines and configurations of the palm of the hand is an important part of the art. In light of my theory, could it be possible that palmists are able to recognise the same characteristics by observing the patterns in our hands? This would be consistent with different races evolving from different tree species at different times. If this could be proven, it would mean that this craft has endured for thousands of years, being passed down through countless generations primarily through word of mouth. This would be an extraordinary outcome, but one that is not an isolated situation. In his book, *The Edge of Memory*, Patrick Nunn gives examples of stories from First Australians that bear truths dating back 10,000 years, all conveyed by word of mouth from one generation to the next. The practice of *palmistree* is widespread across the world, with numerous cultural variations. It is likely that it originated in the Pacific Islands, so it is possible all native Hawaiians, Samoans, Tongans, Tahitians and Maoris evolved from *palmistrees*. Interesting, yet puzzling, is that I have not been able to find out why we call this part of our hand the palm! There is plenty of information that confirms the word for palm trees came about because the base of some palm trees replicates the shape of a human hand. Perhaps this is another reminder of tree ancestors influencing our language, trying to show us this thinking is incorrect, and it is our palms that look like fronds of tropical trees – not the other way round.

pageantree

pageantry; '1 elaborate or sumptuous show or display. 2 an instance of this.'

Includes: Show business promotors and hosts, pageant organisers, pop singers and pop band stage and lighting managers, entertainers and television hosts.

Additional information: Being mindful of not wanting to cross any politically incorrect lines, I think it fair to say that many lesbian, gay, bisexual and transgender humans have strong links to *pageantrees*.

This can be seen in Australia each year in all the spectacular glory of the Sydney Mardi Gras and the Moomba Festival in Victoria. The participants are most likely to be descendants of deciduous trees that are at their most spectacular when in blossom in spring and again in autumn, when their leaves change colour. The powerful genetic forces that guide humans to particular occupations can often be observed in those descended from this species, with them often seeking work as airline stewards, perhaps influenced with the additional mixture in their DNA of planetrees!

paltree

paltry; 'worthless; contemptible, trifling.'

Additional information: This undesirable species affects humans like a cancer of the mind. The effects of *paltrees* can be noticed in humans who focus and worry over minor issues in life, have low self-esteem, always focus on the negative of a situation, and are always hyper-critical of other people and their ideas. They are invariably mean-spirited. I remember a story told to me many years ago about one such character who lived an isolated life in the outback of Australia. Whether or not it was a family member or a good samaritan, I do not recall, but they thought they would try something to help him overcome his extreme pessimism. Knowing that he had never seen a steam engine they took him to a train station to watch as one was about to depart the platform, explaining what it was about to do. As they waited, the pessimist remarked, 'She'll never move.' As it slowly moved off and gathered speed, his benefactor said, 'What do you think now?' His response was, 'She'll never stop!' Throw in a liberal dash of *budgetree* DNA and you have the classic miser mentality (these are the ones who always pay less than their fair share at group dinners in restaurants and always weasel out of shouting a round at the bar). Many end up as recluses. Hopefully, a vaccine will be developed in the future that contains balancing genes from other species to override the dominance of those afflicted with this unfortunate fate.

pantree

pantry; '1 a small room or cupboard in which crockery, cutlery, table linen, etc. are kept. 2 a larder.'

Additional information: Pantrees would have developed early in the evolution of humans, as food and resources would have been as scarce as they were precious. They most likely evolved from forest ancestors in Europe, where the cold winters would allow food storage without perishing. An extreme characteristic of humans who have a strong link to this species manifests in those who become hoarders. Squirrels are no doubt mammals that are related species.

Nearest related type: possibly a close relative of inventrees.

parliamentrees

parliamentary; '1 of or relating to a parliament; 2 enacted or established by parliament. 3 (of language) admissible in a parliament; polite.'

Includes: political ministers, politicians, mayors, local government councillors.

Additional information: This may be stretching things a little, but our tree ancestors may have had an influence on the foundation of one of Britain's political parties. As an outsider to the workings of British politics and bearing in mind what this book is all about, the name 'Tories', when pronounced, almost sounds like 'trees'. Founded in 1834, the party was formed to promote conservatism and British unionism. They believed in divine right, the King's prerogative and *hereditree* succession. The name of the party seems to me an apt fit with these beliefs.

Nearest related types: bigatrees, hortatrees and oratrees.

pastrees

pastries; '1 a dough of flour, fat, and water baked and used as a base and covering for pies, etc.'

Additional information: Although bakers come to mind here, it is likely that these trees evolved to provide a sap-like liquid or paste to sustain the lives of other evolving human species. These trees could have been the forebears of human nursing mothers. This thought may hopefully elicit pride in those working in the bakery *industree*.

perfunctree

perfunctory; '1a done merely for the sake of getting through a duty. b done in a cursory or careless manner. 2 superficial; mechanical.'

Additional information: All humans have their faults, so it is inevitable that not all tree species pass on only good characteristics. Like *hortatrees* and *idolatrees*, this could be one of them. Symptoms of people affected by this genetic link could range from a 'couldn't care less' attitude, to a lack of motivation and drive, but also encompasses those who are just plain lazy. Not surprisingly, they tend to gravitate to benevolent social security systems if they can't keep sponging off their parents. There is, of course, the other scenario as mentioned earlier, where these trees were highly scented species leading to the perfume industry we have today.

Nearest related types: sultrees, amatrees and adultrees. Those imbued with this gene and paltree genes have not been dealt a good hand by nature.

pituitree

pituitary; 'a pea-sized ductless gland at the base of the brain which secretes various hormones essential for growth and other bodily functions'.

Additional information: I am at a loss to understand how this tree type came into being or what its closest tree relative may be. Another *mystree* waiting to be discovered by appropriate researchers.

planetree

planetary; '1 of or like planets; (planetary influence). 2 terrestrial; mundane.'

Nearest related types: undoubtedly observatrees and interplanetrees.

podiatree

podiatry; 'the investigation and treatment of foot disorders'.

Includes: podiatrists obviously have the strongest links here. Footwear manufacturers and pedicurists are influenced by this species, as to a lesser extent are sock manufacturers and nail fungicide and polish makers.

poetree

poetry; '1 the art or work of a poet. 2 poems collectively. 3 a poetic or tenderly pleasing quality.' A rhythmical composition, written or spoken for exciting pleasure by beautiful, imaginative or elevated thoughts.

Additional information: As one of the last trees to take human form once speech became an established means of communication, it should come as no surprise that many of the following evolved from English roots. William Blake, Robert Burns, Lord Byron, Samuel Coleridge and John Keats are names of 18th century English poets known by most of us over the age of 60 from our days learning English at high school. 19th century English poets included Emily Brontë, Elizabeth Browning, Samuel Taylor Coleridge and Rudyard Kipling, with TS Elliot, Wilfred Owens and Dylan Thomas coming to fame in the 20th Century. It is probable this type was very much alive and active before the 18th century, but their prominence only rose with the industrial revolution, when education improved, and most importantly, because the availability of writing materials and books meant that their words could reach a greater audience. I may be way offline, but I suspect a great irony with this genus in that the very medium that helped their stature in society grow is now eroding their relevance in today's world. With the rapid development in computer technologies and the plethora of means of communication this brings – through email, Instagram, Facebook, X (formerly known as Twitter) and mobile phones – I suspect the significance and relevance of poetry could diminish and eventually be consigned to *histree* along with the horse and cart. That said, at the time of writing, a quick look at 'poetry societies' on Google pops up 7,660,000 sites, indicating this tree type will be around for a while yet. I can't help the feeling that some suppressed souls from this genus find expression through writing clues for cryptic crosswords. If you are someone who can figure these out, chances are you have some *poetree ancestree.* I am certain that when an accurate genetic process for matching our DNA with our tree ancestors becomes available, mine would show I have absolutely none!

pottree

pottery; '1 vessels etc. made of fired clay; 2 a potters work. 3 a potters workshop.'

Additional information: The oldest pottery fragment was found in a Chinese cave and has been dated as being 20,000 years old. The oldest potter's wheel dates back to sometime between 4,000 and 6,000 BC, so we know the process is very old. Just when and why the name pottery was designated to this process is a *mystree.* I can only surmise that it may have come from trees that had hollows in them for *rudimentree* storage or food preparation by early tree descendants.

Potter is also a well-known surname, which rose to prominence in England from its beginnings in the 16th century. With the marvels of Google, we can quickly learn that there are over 176,000 people worldwide with this surname. Of interest is the spread of Potters around the world. As the word has English origins, it comes as no surprise that the highest concentration of Potters in Britain come from English counties, with over 31,000. What is surprising is that 94,00 people in the USA have the name Potter. The ratio of Potters to the overall population in the USA to that in the UK, is nearly three to one. This seems extraordinary. Could this be due to large numbers of Potters fleeing some form of persecution in their homeland? That possibility could be the reason why there are over 850 recorded Potters living in Brazil, over 19,000 in Puerto Rico, 7,800 in Canada, 11,400 in Australia and believe it or not, over 500 in Russia! Perhaps the reason could have been the shortage of earthenware makers in the new world that required potters? Perhaps they just breed better in America! Or is it just possible that many Americans have been spellbound by JK Rowling's Harry Potter books and films and had their names changed by deed poll? On that note, one notable Irishman with the Potter surname was Joseph Potter (1828–1873), who was an author and professor at All Hallows College. I can't help but wonder if there is a connection between him and the famous author of Potter fame. This may be stretching things a little, but it is just possible that JK Rowling may have this species as a part of her genetic make-up! After all, the surname Potter is the 209th ranked most common surname in Britain, so there were plenty of more popular names her hero could have been named. There is the slight possibility that the definition of pottery is misleading us from the real nature of this tree type. The prefix 'pot' may in fact reveal that this tree has more to do with hallucinogenic drug properties than earthenware!

predatree

predatory; '1 (of an animal) preying naturally upon others 2 ruthlessly acquisitive, exploitative; aggressive in business etc.'

Additional information: In the evolution of humans from our tree ancestors, it was always going to be just a matter of time before the new humans began fighting over land, food, sex and the right to be the dominant species. Sadly, in many parts of our world this is where evolution seems to have stalled. The means and methods whereby the fighting takes place have 'advanced' due to technology, but the flaws in our basic nature are still essentially the same. Add greed, wealth and religious differences to the initial driving forces, and it could be argued that humans as a race are de-evolving (if that isn't a word then hopefully it will be from now on). Throughout recorded *histree* there have always been murderers, thieves, pirates, despots, and those who, for whatever reason, have a *momentree* reversal to their basic instinct and commit a *predatree* crime. *Predatree* descendants today can be seen en masse in burgeoning jails across the world. Perhaps the vast quantity of media exposure highlighting real life and fictional examples of the *predatree* side of humanity gives one the distinct feeling the world is an extremely dangerous place. The advancements in communications technology that enable one to instantly review details on any topic imaginable seems to me to be a way of eliciting more bizarre and macabre *predatree* behaviour. No echelon of civilized society is free from *predatree* behaviour. From the pillars of governments and the top levels of religious orders to drug lords and their pushers, no sector of society is safe. Cyberbullies, terrorists, perverts, paedophiles and telemarketers all have higher than average levels of this genus in them. Perhaps one day, scientists will be able to extract a gene from the descendants of the original *predatree*, which will enable an elixir or vaccination to be produced and administered to negate the dominance of this gene in susceptible humans. Now, before I move on and we all become despondent about what a crappy world we live in, there is one small but nonetheless noteworthy benefit to the spread of civilisation that may bring comfort to those who find difficulty sleeping at night, due to the weight of all this negativity. Progress has at least been made in many parts of the world with primitive societies to dramatically reduce the extremely *predatree* practice of cannibalism!

proprietree

proprietary; '1a of, holding, or concerning property (the proprietary classes). b of or relating to a proprietor (proprietary rights). 2 held in private ownership; (of a product, esp. a drug or medicine) marked under and protected by a registered trade name.'

Includes: real estate agents, conveyancers, surveyors, perhaps.

Additional information: The second part of the definition is a recent addition to the meaning and has nothing to do with the purpose of the original trees. While it is not the key topic for discussion here, as discussed below, it is interesting to note another example of how words and their meanings change over time. It is the words 'relating to property or ownership' that are the clue to the evolution of these trees. It is probable that this species evolved from the need to have an umpire of sorts to adjudicate which trees belonged to which section of land to prevent or mitigate arguments between species. It is possible that their legacy lives on today in those who have an earnest desire to work in the following fields: police, security, border defence in the armed forces, and even umpires and referees in all manner of sports. The name itself suggests a high level of ethical and moral standards, as the 'proper' implies. Sadly, over time, things change, and these trees succumbed to the pressures of their high office and the temptations that would have been placed in front of them, so that today, the directors and

CEOs descended from them use the term *proprietree* 'limited' as a way of trying to convince people that they are trustworthy enterprises. The often-added word 'limited' means that the *proprietree* company is limited in its liability – it is so comforting to know that there are such ethical businesses out there that have self-imposed standards on limiting their ability to lie, fib, tell porky pies, etc.

Nearest related types: territrees and countrees.

psychiatree

psychiatry; 'the study and treatment of mental disease.'

Includes: psychologists, psychiatrists, astrologers, mediums, soothsayers, motivational speakers, hypnotists and tea leaf readers, perhaps. This trait has been discussed in the chapter The Theory of Treevolution and Medicine.

purgatree

purgatory; '1 the condition, or supposed place of spiritual cleansing, esp. of those who die in the grace of god but have to expiate venial sins etc. 2 a place or state of temporary suffering, or expiation.'

Additional information: Related to *ministrees*, it is arguable whether these trees were their henchmen, tasked with hunting out the sinner trees that had transgressed somehow, or if this was the name given to trees that, for some reason or other, were considered to be undesirable within the species. This trait has been discussed in the chapter, The Theory of Treevolution and Religion.

respiratree

respiratory; 'relating to or affecting respiration of the organs of respiration.'

Additional information: this trait has been discussed in the chapter The Theory of Treevolution and Medicine.

reformatrees

reformatory; 'serving or designed to reform; a penal institution for the reformation of young offenders'.

Includes: Judges, prison wardens, prison guards, police, foster parents, some political aspirants and do-gooders in general. These trees no doubt evolved to intervene in deviant behaviour of young trees that were breaking *forestree* rules. It is only in recent years that this term for institutions that deal with wayward human adolescents has been changed. By their very nature, *reformatrees* are involved primarily with *purgatrees*, but they are not directly related. It is possible this genus has an offshoot species that reforms trees in a physical way. Descendants of this sub-species may be given to indulging in topiary, pruning and otherwise shaping trees.

refractree

refractory; '1 stubborn, unmanageable, rebellious.'

Additional information: A general trait of most two-year old human infants that, in most cases, fortunately loses its influence as other genetic traits take precedence. In severe cases, the effects of this species can endure into adulthood, as many an employee would have experienced with a superior or boss at some time or other. A classic example of an excess of this species DNA manifesting in a human is readily observable in several leaders (at the time of writing) of world superpowers.

Nearest related types: bigatrees, derogatrees and condemnatrees.

registree

registry; '1 a place or office where registers or records are kept. 2 registration.'

Includes: generally, people who work in government departments keeping records, librarians, census collectors, sports statisticians and those people who cross off your name at polling booths during elections.

Nearest related types: countrees, repositrees, budgetrees, depositrees and pantrees.

repositree

repository; '1 a place where things are stored or may be found, esp. a warehouse or museum. 2 a receptacle.'

Includes: squirrels and chipmunks are two mammals that store nuts, acorns and berries and are thus related to this species, as are, no doubt, many species of birds.

Nearest related types: budgetrees, depositrees, pantrees and countrees.

rotree

rotary; 'acting by rotation (rotary drill; rotary pump).'

Additional information: Lance Hill, the Australian inventor of the famous Hill's Hoist clothesline and German Felix Wankel, who invented the rotary motor engine, are obvious descendants, as no doubt were the inventors of the wheel. Perhaps those who set up and who are attracted to that wonderful *voluntree* group, Rotary, are also influenced, if not descended, from this species. On the other hand, as the above definition implies, the union of *rotrees* with an axis or pivot point, could this mean that the leaders of Germany, Italy and Japan who banded together to instigate World War II became known as the Axis Powers, because of their descendancy from *rotrees*?

rudimentree

rudimentary; '1 involving basic principles; fundamental. 2 incompletely developed; vestigial, relating to an immature, undeveloped or basic form'.

Additional information: No doubt related to *elementrees*, I suspect that *rudimentrees* were most likely the first breakaway species from our tree ancestors. Adam and Eve (T1 and T2) would most definitely have been *rude-imentrees*, at least until they learned how to adorn themselves with fig leaves, so it is possible the name encompasses the nakedness of these first trees. When I was a child the term 'rudie' or 'rudie nudie' were commonly used when we were naked, usually after a bath. Sadly, as we have seen with so many other words and expressions, the term has all but disappeared and with it, another link to our origins is lost. The evidence in the words, immature, undeveloped or basic form in the definition above, can clearly be seen from the behaviours of many young males, particularly during their teenage years. A typical example of this is young males who do burnouts in their cars on public roads and think this behaviour somehow makes them look 'cool.'

salutree

salutary; '1 producing good effects; beneficial, 2 archaic health giving, advantageous, good, profitable, productive, helpful, useful, valuable, worthwhile, timely'.

Additional information: In general terms, a good dose of this species in humans is beneficial.

Nearest related type: these trees may be related to *militrees*, given all the saluting that goes on in the armed forces.

sanitree

sanitary; '1 of the conditions that affect health, esp. with regard to dirt and infection. 2 hygienic; free from or designed to kill germs, infection etc.'

Includes: health inspectors, doctors, nurses, manufacturers of germ-killing products, *sanitree* products, air dryers in public loos, etc.

Additional information: The importance of this genetic trait could be seen in those courageous front-line medical professionals who dealt with the coronavirus epidemic. It is highly likely that a close descendant of the *sanitree*, is the sanity. We are most fortunate that today in Australia and most of the western world, through the advances in medical science we have never experienced the raft of terrible diseases that have decimated human populations over the ages. Polio, tuberculosis, cholera, diphtheria, tetanus, leprosy, malaria, typhoid, hepatitis, rubella, syphilis and gonorrhoea are just some of the diseases that threatened the survival of our ancestors. Apart from the physical suffering, there was also the mental aspect these diseases inflicted. Many of these diseases could make their victims go mad. As discussed earlier, trees come under attack from all sorts of parasites and pests above and below ground. it's no wonder those afflicted probably lost their sanity, albeit at a very slow pace, hence the evolution of *sanitees* from the parent species, *sanitrees.*

satisfactree

satisfactory; '1 adequate; causing or giving satisfaction; (was a satisfactory pupil).

2 satisfying expectations or needs; leaving no room for complaint (a satisfactory result).'

Additional information: This type has imbued humans with the desirable character traits of tranquillity, contentment, positive self-esteem, acceptance and satisfaction. Sadly, for him, and despite his considerable fame and success, the Rolling Stones lead singer, Mick Jagger was one who lamented his lack of genetic inheritance from this tree type, through the lyrics of one of his hits in 1965 ('I can't get no satisfaction').

Nearest related type: complementrees.

secretree

secretary; '1 a person employed by an individual or in an office etc. to assist with correspondence, keep records, make appointments, etc. 2 an official appointed by a society etc. to conduct its correspondence, keep its records, organise its affairs etc.'

Includes: secretaries, spies, FBI agents.

Additional information: The word no doubt relates to the ability of these trees to keep secrets. Some people can be trusted with information they have received in confidence. However, almost everyone knows someone who promises to keep a secret, but in fact tells someone else as soon as possible. It is well documented that a strong genetic mix of *secretree* and *sultree* DNA in women can create personal dilemmas for rich men and politicians.

sedentree

sedentary; '1 sitting (a sedentary posture). 2 (of work etc.) characterised by much sitting and little physical exercise. 3 (of a person) spending much time seated. Zoo. a inhabiting the same locality throughout life; non-migratory. b confined to one spot; sessile.'

Additional information: As you read the last lines of this definition, I can almost guarantee that you instantly thought of someone or some creature you know that fits the description of a *sedentree*. Predominantly (but not exclusively), males of the human race who are generally overweight and attached to the television remote are the epitome of this reversion to an ancestral type. The dramatic changes in living standards and lifestyles, particularly in the western world, has caused a huge number of humans to be sucked back to their ancestral roots of this species. In truth, due to their very nature, all our tree ancestors had this gene – being rooted in the one place for life. If they hadn't, they probably would have all gone mad. So, all humans have a degree of this *sedentree* gene in their genetic make-up.

In historical terms, up until the recent past (say 100 years ago), life for our forebears was often very difficult, both physically and mentally. The life expectancy for Australians born between 1901 and 1910 was 49.5 years and 54.8 years for men and women, respectively. Tough living and working conditions for people up until these times meant most died before any *sedentree* influences could take effect. One hundred years later, men born in 2012–14 can expect to reach 80.3 and women born in the same period will reach 84.4, which is a significant increase. This increased life expectancy, combined with decreased pressures to fulfil the basic needs of housing, safety, and finding and preparing food, have increased the conditions that lead to the growth of *sedentree* behaviours. Then there are the dramatic changes in what actually passes for food these days, which is far removed from what the human digestive system was designed to process. With all this in mind, it is no wonder that, despite the best efforts of medical science and gains in some areas, overall, conditions such as heart disease, cancers of all types and diabetes have been increasing in numbers each year. On a lighter note, I suspect that stationarees are, or were, an offshoot species to *sedentrees*. It is likely the name derived from the suitability of the timber for paper production rather than the fact that they were easier for *predatrees* to catch!

sedimentree

sedimentary; '1 of or like sediment. 2 Geol. (esp.of rocks) formed from sediment.'

Includes: geologists and perhaps archaeologists have strong links with this tree type.

Additional information: Parents who have this gene often call their sons 'Rock', or their kids tend to gravitate to the music genre of the same name. A hint of *sedimentree* influence can be observed in youths, mainly boys, who have an urge to throw stones. From a medical perspective, people who get gall, kidney and calcium stones probably have proportionately higher levels of this genetic strain than the average population.

Nearest related species: I suspect that there is most likely a link with cemetrees here, but just in what way is another mystree.

sentree

sentry; 'a soldier etc. stationed to keep guard.'

Includes: militree guards, bodyguards, security guards, bouncers perhaps. All dogs, particularly guard dogs, share ancestral links to this type. This explains why there is such a strong bond between security personnel and the guard dogs they work with.

Nearest related type: militrees.

solitree

solitary; '1 living alone; not gregarious; without companions; lonely (a solitary existence). 2 (of a place) secluded or unfrequented. 3 single or sole. (a solitary instance).'

Includes: hermits, lighthouse keepers, lepers.

Nearest related type: possibly related to purgatrees that have been exiled.

statutree

statutory; '1 required, permitted or enacted by statute. (statutory minimum; statutory provisions. 2 (of a criminal offence) carrying a penalty prescribed by statute.'

Additional information: Although the current meanings of the word bear no meaning to this next point, it is probable that all of the famed statues throughout the world were produced by humans descended from statue-trees. In days long past, master sculptors acknowledged our tree ancestors with this word. By making a solid replica of a person, they were perpetuating a human in a stationary tree form.

Nearest related type: cemetrees.

sultree

sultry; '1 (of the atmosphere or the weather) hot or oppressive; close. 2 (of a person, character, etc.) passionate; sensual.'

Includes: female night club singers, pole dancers, some female movie stars (think Marylin Monroe), and prostitutes.

Nearest related types: most likely amatrees, adultrees and purgatrees.

suppositrees

suppositories; 'a medical preparation in the form of a cone, cylinder, etc. to be inserted into the rectum or vagina to dissolve.'

Additional information: I suspect if this was an actual tree type, they must have been very small and their application for medical purposes rather unpleasant! This type is mentioned in the chapter on The Theory of Treevolution and Medicine.

symmetree

symmetry; '1a correct proportion of the parts of a thing; balance, harmony. b beauty resulting from this.'

Additional information: For the interest of those who follow astrology, most Librans exhibit these traits.

tapestree

tapestry; '1a a textile fabric in which coloured weft threads are woven to form pictures or designs.'

Additional information: The naming of this tree probably derived from patterns on its bark. Influencing effects of this species manifest in those involved in the textile industry to individuals who love to weave, knit, crochet, etc. These days, modern machinery does much of the work previously done by people working independently in their homes. The legacy of the work carried out by these generations of *tapestrees* in keeping the rest of humanity warm cannot be underestimated. I do not wish to tarnish the image of those descended from *tapestrees*, but there is a possibility the sap obtained through the 'tap' in these trees may have had a strong narcotic effect, which could give rise to all the patterns and vivid colours these people see. It would be interesting to study descendants of *tapestrees* to determine if there are higher incidences of recreational drug use and addiction. Perhaps this could be a project for an enterprising university student doing their postgraduate thesis – if a strong correlation was to be found, a cure would surely follow. I hope the prospect of instant fame and the possibility of a Nobel Prize nomination is taken up soon. No doubt, Sir Richard Arkwright, who developed the spinning machine, is a good example of someone who had strong *tapestree* influences that were balanced by *inventree* and *industree* genes. I suspect most Scottish people have elevated levels of this gene, as evidenced in the tartan patterns of their kilts and bagpipes.

territree

territory; '1 the extent of the land under the jurisdiction of a ruler, state, city, etc. 2 (also Territory) an organised division of a country, esp. one not yet admitted to the full rights of a state.'

Additional information: this tree type is discussed in the chapter The Theory of Treevolution and The Origins of Armed Forces.

Nearest related types: sentrees, predatrees, militrees and countrees.

transitree

transitory; 'not permanent, brief, transient.'

Includes: Human descendants may be those who have trouble
making and keeping commitments or settling down, or who are always
looking for the next adventure. It is likely that all humans possess
some of this species. We will all exit life at some point, and a human
lifespan is but a blink of an eye when viewed against the abyss of time.
Perhaps this genetic strain guides people to transit *industrees* – truckies,
bus drivers, couriers, postal delivery workers.

Nearest related type: as the definition states, these trees are (or were)
closely related to momentrees.

tributree

tributary; '1 a river or stream flowing into a larger river or lake. 2
hist. a person or state paying or subject to tribute.'

Additional information: It is unclear if this species is so named
because of its dependence on freshwater flows or if they are related
to *complimentrees* who pay tributes. Perhaps today's descendants are those
who work out who is worthy of receiving medals, commendations,
awards and the like. If so, Queen Elizabeth – or someone on her staff
– must have had a decent dose of this gene, considering the number
and diversity of recipients and gongs awarded through Her Birthday
Honours lists. Another possibility, of course, is that the name relates
to the desirable characteristics of serenity. Descendants with a liberal
sprinkling of this may be those people who never seem to be stressed
– in keeping with the definition of a flowing stream they just go with
the flow of life – the 'que sera sera' set. On the other hand, there is a
less desirable possibility that these people could be the drifters in life,
never able to put down roots and settle in one place for long.

unsatisfactree

unsatisfactory; the evil twin of *satisfactrees*! '1 not satisfactory; poor, unacceptable.'

Additional information: This species probably evolved to offset *satisfactrees* from becoming too complacent and too accepting, thereby becoming meek and mild, able to be pushed around and bullied, and liable to become extinct. Unfortunately, just as weeds will take over the most carefully laid out gardens over time, *unsatisfactrees* appear to be the dominant of the two species. We all know at least one of these glass-half empty, over-critical, nit-picking, never satisfied, never giving a compliment, always ready to snuff the life out of someone's idea by immediately verbalising why it's a stupid one, type of person. *Unsatisfactrees* may often be over-achievers, always striving for perfection, yet rarely experiencing anything approaching joy. Just as some people can drink quite a bit of alcohol and still appear sober, others can quickly become two-pot screamers. As with most things in life, it's a delicate balance.

Nearest related species: possibly derogatrees, bigatrees, condemnatrees, contradictrees, hortatrees and inflammatrees.

uncomplimentree

uncomplimentary; 'not complimentary, insulting. the evil twin of *complimentrees*'.

Nearest related type: derogatrees.

upholstree

upholstery; '1 textile covering, padding, springs, etc. for furniture. 2 an upholsterer's work.'

Additional information: This species of tree was probably focused on depth, colour and tactility of bark texture, with these traits surfacing in those people in industrees related to clothing apparel, carpet and rug makers, and bedding manufacturers. Cork trees may be associated with *upholstrees*.

Nearest related type: close relatives of tapestrees.

valedictree

valedictory; 'serving as a farewell, a farewell address."

Additional information: Possibly a term for very old trees that were about to die, or more optimistically, a graduation reference to young trees as they left their parent tree as new mobile humans.

Nearest related type: laudatrees, complimentrees and possibly cemetrees.

vestree

vestry; '1 a room or a building attached to a church for keeping vestments. 2 hist.a meeting of parishioners, usu. in a vestry, for parochial business. b a body of parishioners meeting in this way.'

Additional information: When I came across this tree, I had no idea what a *vestree* was. My interest was heightened when my enquiries as to its meaning mentioned a place where vestments are kept. Being the simple pagan that I am, I assumed that vestments must be related to investments and so *vestrees* must be a church's equivalent to a bank (I always wondered where the church stashed the cash collected on that gold plate passed around at Sunday school). To my disappointment, the meaning of vestment (a garment, especially a ceremonial or office robe, or a robe worn by the clergy or choristers during services) was somewhat of a letdown. *Vestrees* probably started out as simple tailors, making vests for early humans to presumably help keep them warm. Today's descendants can be found plying their trade anywhere from the sweatshops of third world countrees to the fashion catwalks of the world. I still cling to the notion that *vestrees* are in fact the church's coffers and the robes are just a smokescreen to hide this. Irrespective of any *monetree* connection, having seen enough of these gold-inlaid and ornately designed vestments in churches on a trip to Europe made me realise just how much *monetree* worth is possibly tied up in these *vestrees*.

victree

victory; '1 the process of defeating an enemy in battle or war, or an opponent in a contest 2 an instance of this.'

Additional information: As with *predatrees*, humans need a liberal dose of this species in their genetic make-up if they are to be successful. Too little and people can become stereotyped as losers; people with too much have a win-at-all-costs attitude and usually cross a line that eventually sees them fall from grace. Politics and sport are two areas littered with famous individuals who have cheated to win and been found out, with the inevitable slide into ignominy. It is interesting to note that the opposite of *victree* is defeat. It is comforting to know that civilization has at least advanced to the level whereby we can keep the original word and meaning of defeat, but the victors no longer feel the need to chop off people's feet if they lose!

voluntree

voluntary; '1 done, acting, or able to act of one's own free will; not constrained or compulsory; intentional (a voluntary gift). 2 unpaid (voluntary work).'

Additional information: Where would the human world be without the countless people who volunteer their time for so many varied and important activities? Every human should have a liberal dose of this species in their genetic make-up. I would go so far as to say that if the genes of this tree can be isolated, they could be added to the childhood vaccination programs that prevent the known serious diseases. I am certain then, that the incidences of suicide, self-harm, depression and unhappiness that we hear of with increasing frequency, would decrease. *Voluntrees* are the keepers of at least one of the keys to human happiness and success. Some people never learn that one of life's greatest lessons is that it's not what you get in life that is important, but what you give back, that ultimately sets one's mind free.

wintree

wintry; '1 characteristic of winter (wintry weather; a wintry sun; a wintry landscape). 2 (of a smile, greeting etc.) lacking warmth or enthusiasm.'

Additional information: These were most likely trees that evolved in very cold climates. Given that we now know the earth has been through a few ice ages, they must be from tough stock. Only people descended from these species would choose to live in the colder regions of our world. Alternatively, there is the chance that *wintrees* were trees that were overly competitive, wanting to win at all costs. We all know someone who has an overabundance of this trait. If so, they are most likely related to *victrees*.

watree

watery; '1 containing too much water. 2 too thin in consistency. 3 of or consisting of water.'

Additional information: An appropriate tree word to end this chapter. In support of my theory, I pose this question. Can it be mere coincidence that both humans and trees are composed mainly of water?

※·≈·❧·≈·※

This completes the list of all of the various trees with their vocational and other forces that guided you into your working life and all those trees that may have influenced how your nature was formed. By now, you are most likely wondering which species and what percentage mix of trees best represents you, your partner, your children and quite possibly, your boss. This analysis can sometimes be difficult, as we often see ourselves quite differently from other people's perspectives.

Personally, I found it easier to eliminate those species that I felt certain had no influence over me, then share my findings with my lifelong partner, who knows me much better than I know myself. My self-assessment identified the following species:

- *conservatree* – a fundamental drive in writing this book

- *voluntree* – I volunteer for the bush care programs in a large national park near Adelaide

- *elementree* – I am a basic male, as outlined in my introduction

- *exploratree* – always happy to go down a road I haven't been on before – this book for one

- *solitree* – I enjoy the company of others, but I am also quite content to have time alone

- *satisfactree* – Librans are easy to please

- *predatree* – everyone needs a percentage of this species to survive, and I doubt I could ever be a vegan

- *momentree* – apparently, I have the attention span of a spanner, but hopefully will live long enough to finish this book

- *complimentree* – I am mindful of paying them if they are warranted

- *symmetree* – in line with my astrological profile

- *dormitree* – consistent with my hair loss, confirming my deciduous ancestry, and my difficulty in getting up early on wintry mornings.

THE A TO Z OF TY WORDS

❧❧❧✦❧❧❧

There is no doubt that we humans are at the top of the proverbial food chain thanks to our tree ancestors. With our larger brain size and the ability to use our hands and fingers we can create, make and do things that no other animal can. Evolution has been kind to us, and I am reminded of this whenever I watch a David Attenborough *documentree* on the struggles faced by the various creatures with which we share our planet. A favourite example of this is the relatively recent filming of a harlequin tuskfish using a rock to crack open a clam underwater. A key question that now arises is: why do humans do the things they do?

Putting aside the activities essential to providing the basic needs for survival, what compels humans to create music, paint masterpieces, climb mountains, jump from planes hoping a parachute will save them, include curling as a sport in the Olympic Games and so on? From earlier chapters we know trees have given humans – and most other mammals evolved from them – a caring and nurturing nature. However, as far as I am aware, there are few animals on the planet that exhibit behaviours other than what they naturally need to do to survive and breed. We all know that cats purr when content and dolphins seem to do things for fun, as do dogs, and I am sure there are more examples. My wife and I have a much-loved dog, and on occasion, he shows a reasonable amount of intelligence. Yet, despite his privileged life of luxury, free from the rigours of having to fend for himself, with plenty of time to ponder the universe and his existence, he shows no signs or urges to be anything or do anything other than what a dog is and does.

It took quite a time for me to realise that the primary driver of human endeavour is emotion. Now I admit that this is a difficult area for me to discuss (and I suspect most men of my post-Neanderthalic era are no different). It has only been in recent years that I have come to understand that the word relates predominantly to human feelings. I say this because prior to this dawning awareness, I presumed an e-motion was something that happened just prior to you trying to access your e-mail. This was based on my theory that the internet is overloaded with too much data and needs time off for the equivalent of a rather large informational bowel motion, somewhere up in some poor unsuspecting cloud.

This confession aside, if I am correct with my new assumption, the question then arises: from where did these emotions come? Could they have been passed down by our tree ancestors, or are emotions a later development that grew from our interactions with the world around us after we had well and truly broken the umbilical cord? A search through various channels has not revealed a clear answer to this question. The scientific answer is basically that a tree has no brain, so cannot register pain or feelings. On the other hand, the sheer weight of numbers of people who would disagree with the science 'know' that trees definitely have feelings and therefore must have at least some sort of primitive emotion.

Eventually, I realised I was not only barking up the wrong tree in search of the answer, but I also just couldn't see the wood for the trees. The whole premise of the theory of treevolution is anchored by clues left in the English language, yet of all the 'tree' words listed in the previous chapters, most relate to behavioural and vocational outcomes. Few if any, have any connotation with emotions. So, I began scrolling through the English vocabulary again, with a different mindset and what I found was there are over 300 words in the English language that have 'ty' as the last two letters. I surmise that many of these words ending in 'ty', which is close to 'try', and therefore 'tree', are related to emotions. Most of them relate to all aspects of human nature, human character and human–life interactions, with some indicating feelings or emotions. Admittedly, this is only a small percentage, but this is logical, as our original ancestors would not have had the brain development or the need for emotions – at least up until they began evolving mammals and birds. The pattern of spelling, the number of these words and their emotional meaning is enough to convince me that trees have feelings – we just do not yet have a way to scientifically prove it. These feelings probably developed in response to the separation of the first trees (T1 and T2) as they stumbled off to make their way in the world. As part of this theory, the following lists many of these words, with comments where I feel they are warranted, and I have marked those which indicate emotions in bold.

ability; amity; abnormality; absurdity; accountability; actuality; adversity; affability; affinity; alacrity; almighty (perhaps in deference to the Tree of Knowledge, if not God him/herself); ambiguity; amenity; amnesty; amity; antiquity; **anxiety** (obviously in relation to *psychiatrees*); aplenty; asperity; atrocity; audacity; authority.

barbarity; batty; bestiality; beauty; bitty; booty; bounty; brevity (*momentrees* perhaps); busty (probably comes from *sultrees* or *amatrees*).

calamity; captivity; casualty; catty; cavity; certainty; chastity; chatty; civility; clarity; **combustibility** (probably relates to *inflammatrees*), commodity; community; compatibility; complexity; complicity; continuity; conviviality; county (a sibling of *countree*); credibility; cruelty; crusty; cupidity; curiosity.

dainty; debility; deity (cousins of *bigatrees* perhaps); deformity; density; depravity; **desirability**; dignity; disability; dirty; discontinuity; dishonesty; disloyalty; disparity; diversity; dotty; doughty; durability; duplicity; dusty; duty; dynasty.

eccentricity; elasticity; electricity; **emotionality**; empty; **enmity**; enormity; equanimity; equity; eternity (anyone care for a game of cricket?); eventuality; extremity.

falsity; fatality; faulty; **felicity**; femininity; ferocity; fertility; festivity; fidgety; **fidelity**; finality; flighty; fragility; frailty; fraternity; frivolity; frosty; frowsty; fruity; fusty; futility.

gaiety; garrulity; generality; generosity; gentility (related to *gentrees*); gratuity; gravity (one of the first lessons to be learned by our first descendants was that any attempts to defy gravity would never turn out well. In my case, the first such lesson learned was to always wear sturdy shoes when riding my bike); gristly; gusty; gutsy.

hasty; hearty; heredity; hilarity; honesty; hostility; humanity; humility.

identity; immortality; immunity; impartiality; impiety; improbability; impropriety; impunity; impurity; inability; inactivity; incapacity; incivility; incredulity; indemnity; **indignity**; individuality; inequality; inequity; infelicity; **infidelity**; infinity; infirmity; informality; iniquity; **insanity** (what happens to trees when *psychiatrees* fail); **insecurity**; insobriety; instability; integrity; intensity; irregularity (I am sure there were many instances where trialling new foods did not work out well); irritability.

knotty.

legality; legibility; levity; liberty; locality; lofty; loyalty; lusty.

magnanimity; majesty; masculinity; maturity; meaty; mentality; mighty; misty; mobility; modernity; modesty; monstrosity; morality; morbidity; mortality.

naivety; nasty; nationality; nativity; natty; naughty; negativity; nicety; nifty; nonentity; normality; notability; novelty; nutty.

objectivity; obscurity; oddity; opportunity; originality.

parity; party; particularity; partiality; pedantry; penalty; pernickety; perpetuity; perplexity; personality; perversity; pity; plenty; plurality; polarity; possibility; posterity; poverty; practicality; predictability; pretty; priority; probability; proclivity; productivity; profanity; promiscuity; property; propriety; prosperity; proximity; puberty; publicity; punctuality; purity; putty.

quality; quantity.

rarity; ratty; reality; responsibility; rickety; rusty.

safety; sanctity; sanity, scanty; scarcity; security; seniority; sensibility; **sensitivity**; sensuality; serendipity; sexuality; shanty; shifty; similarity; simplicity; sincerity; singularity; solidarity; sophistry; speciality; spirituality; sporty; stability; stupidity; suavity; superiority; surety; sweaty.

tarty; tasty; temerity; tenacity; testy; thirsty; thrifty; throaty; totality; tranquillity; travesty; treaty; triviality; trusty; try; twisty.

uniformity; unity; university; utility.

vanity; variety; velocity; verbosity; vicinity; virginity; virtuosity; vitality; volitivity; virility.

warranty; weighty; witty.

If humans are descended from trees and we inherited our emotional qualities from them, it is likely that other mammalian tree descendants would also exhibit similar behaviours. Books could be written about the myriad ways animals show love and devotion to each other and to humans. Anyone who has owned a pet knows this, so I do not need to elaborate, other than to give one example as to how deeply some animals feel. Grief is the outpouring of pain that comes from the death of a loved one. Anyone who has lost someone they love knows what this feels like and how long it lasts. The grief behaviours of elephants, monkeys, dogs, giraffes, dolphins and many other mammals are well documented. The most prominent non-mammalian creatures showing grief are many species of birds. This should not be a surprise as we have established in previous chapters that most bird species evolved from trees.

Having just waded through this long list, one can be forgiven for the urge to yawn, rest your eyes and mind, or to close this book altogether, so now is probably a good time to reinvigorate your attention with something a little more interesting.

Let's discuss sex.

THE THEORY OF TREEVOLUTION AND SEX

❧❧❧❦❧❧❧

For survival, many creatures rely on their sense of smell to detect threats and find prey. Survival also depends on procreation of the species. In both these respects, humans have a lot in common with trees.

The whole point of plants and trees bursting into blossom is to either attract other species to facilitate pollination, or for the wind to spread its seeds or pollen. With annual worldwide sales for perfumery products for the year 2023 estimated to be US$48.05 billion, the correlation between trees and humans is obvious. The word perfunctory is defined as 'an act performed merely as an uninteresting or routine duty'. However, I surmise that *perfunctrees* may have been highly perfumed trees, whose acts would have been anything other than 'uninteresting or routine', at least to trees. Perhaps the meaning has been reversed to hide the possibility that these trees were a little too seductive!

An overt sexual example linking our tree ancestors to human beings surfaces in those people whose attraction to trees goes beyond just talking to and hugging them. Dendrophilia, sometimes referred to as arborphilia or dendrophily, can become a fetish when humans hugging trees turns to tree petting and sexual arousal. Perhaps these folk are just more in tune with their ancestral origins. The intricacies involved with the varied sexual natures of trees, and their interrelations and co-dependencies on other creatures, are beyond the scope of my work. However, I can say that I now understand where their human offspring developed the sexual practice of orgies.

This brings me to another word that binds us to our tree ancestors. This is the word 'root' and its variations. We all know that a root is a part of the underground structure of a plant or tree that attaches it to the ground and through which the tree draws moisture and nutrients from the soil. In Australia, at least, the word is, or perhaps I should say, was, also used in a slang sense to refer to an act of having or looking to initiate sex. 'Having a good root', 'looking for a root' and 'asking for a root,' were all terms teenagers of my generation were familiar with. These terms have all but died out now, particularly the last one, as the success rate was minimal at best. The word root was gradually displaced by that four-letter word starting with 'f' that was taboo fifty years ago. Before the terms above disappear from histree, I record it here in this work because I feel that its relevance is far more significant than just a slang expression for a sexual act. These words and their meanings intertwine humans and trees in the sense that both trees and a good human marriage require a good rooting system to thrive and be productive!

The character traits of a *sultree* would be similar, with the probable inclusion of the word busty. Both species are no doubt related, the difference being location. The current meaning of sultry is 'oppressively hot and close or moist; characterised by or arousing temper or passion'. So, *sultrees* would have most likely been promiscuous tropical trees. Female night club singers, pole dancers, some female movie stars (think Marylin Monroe) and hookers are probable descendants. *Mystrees* are defined as a 'puzzle, enigma, conundrum, riddle, secret, uncertainty, mystique'. Most women have varying degrees of genetic inheritance from this tree type, and from a man's perspective, the word complexity could well be added. They are related to *amatrees*, *sultrees*, *perfunctrees* and *adultrees*.

Adultrees were probably mature-age trees that engaged in illicit acts of propagation with other species. To the emerging tree-humans struggling for their survival, this could have been seen as an act of betrayal or possible even *treeson*. To this day, acts of betrayal within the human species are held in the highest contempt, none more so than as outlined at the end of the chapter Treevolution and the Origins of Armed Forces. The 'ty' ending words characterising this species are impropriety and impurity, with perhaps a little too much virility.

Small trees that were too young to flower no doubt inspired the words virginity, chastity and puberty.

TREEISMS

❧❧⫘❧❧

I n looking for links binding our tree *ancestree* with our language, it would be remiss of me not to look at some common and many almost-extinct phrases, expressions and words that relate to trees.

It *'wood'* be easy to dismiss most of these expressions as being merely the logical language outcomes of being so intertwined and dependent on trees at the times I have surmised the forests of Europe and Britain began moulding the English language to ensure their legacy would not be forgotten. I *wood* argue that, in the context of the compelling evidence that forms the basis of this book, some of these provide further proof of our tree heritage. For example, people still say when they settle down that they are 'putting down roots', or after having been away for some time, they return to their original home to be 'closer to their roots'. The practical association between the roots anchoring a tree and the desire of humans to remain in one place seem perfectly logical. It is possible there is an underlying truth in these words, in that there is this unconscious ancestral tree force that draws people back to their forest patch and their origins of being planted in or having come from the one place. This force is less subtle than those more dramatic examples of tree man syndrome or of being *petreefied*, but it cannot be discounted.

The common expression 'get wind of', means to become aware of something through indirect means, especially something being kept secret. The term arises from some animals' abilities to become aware of a scent carried in the air. As we are related to many mammals with this ability, and these animals probably descended from trees that we know can detect scents, it is reasonable to suggest humans should also have this ability, albeit to a lesser extent and in a slightly different way. When humans use this term, it is generally not referring to the actual detection of a physical scent. It is more to do with what we feel as a 'hunch', 'vibe' or 'gut feeling'. We usually don't know how we get these feelings, which are sometimes referred to as intuition. Whatever it is, I think we have inherited this ability from our tree ancestors, and they used this process to guide our human forebears in the structure of the English language.

Few people would not be familiar with the term 'winning the wooden spoon' and its associated meaning. The term has British origins and is attributed to coming from the University of Cambridge in the early 1800s. It related to a practice of awarding a wooden spoon as a booby prize to the scholar achieving the lowest score in mathematics exams at the end of each year. I presume the choice of wood may have had something to do with its abundant availability, low cost, and the implication that the unfortunate recipient was as brainless as a tree. As to why a spoon – when you look at the terminology, rules and duration of the game of cricket, which evolved around the same time, there is really not much point in trying to get a rational explanation, so I count this expression out in terms of an association with our forebears. However, in view of the obvious respect I have for trees, I would support any move to have last place awards made of a substance other than wood. Recycled plastic, perhaps. Once enough people grasp the essence of this work, attitudes towards timber will change. It may take some time, but winning the wooden spoon will eventually symbolise first place, with metal awards being relegated to minor placings. Major sporting champions will hoist trophies made from beautifully crafted timbers, possibly coming from trees identified as *victrees*.

Some people are in the unfortunate situation of having 'legs like tree-trunks'. This may be related in some way to a reversionary condition like tree-man syndrome. In medical terminology, the phrase is generally assigned to lipoedema, a painful and incurable genetic condition causing leg swelling due to fat build-up in the limbs. Hopefully, through further study of trees, the cause of this condition will become evident and remedial *treetment* will soon be available.

An almost extinct expression, generally attributed to olden day pirates, is 'shiver me timbers.' The term was an exclamation of surprise or shock, just as Australians use the terms 'well I'll be buggered', 'stone the flamin' crows', 'holy crap' and 'crikey'. There are many more Australian words used in this context – although the shorter exclamations of surprise usually involve well-known one-word profanities and are reserved for more urgent situations, such as opening the washing machine and finding a twelve-foot python curled within. All totally understandable in a country with more deadly creatures that bite, sting and kill than anywhere else on the planet. But I digress. The explanation for the previous expression is that 'shiver' is an old English word meaning 'to break into small fragments or splinters' and most likely alluded to the shock of a large wave or cannonball crashing into a wooden ship, causing the hull to shudder. I suggest the term may have a different origin. Many a sailor was washed overboard from the early wooden boats, often into very cold seas. This would result in cold rapidly setting into the limbs, causing them to shiver. But why would a sailor in this predicament refer to their arms and legs as timber, unless there was a far deeper understanding that could only be evoked in this near-death situation?

While researching expressions involving timber, I came across one that I immediately thought would make an excellent addition to this chapter. My initial thoughts on the wording 'tongue and groove' conjured up titillating visions of nubile young trees cavorting through the forest while simultaneously French-kissing and dancing the jitterbug. You can understand my disappointment then, to find that the term refers to 'wooden planking in which adjacent boards are joined by means of interlocking ridges and hollows down their sides'! What a let-down. Apparently, this common term is understood by most people, particularly those involved in the building and furnishing trades. Understandably, in my tree profile assessment in a previous chapter, I have correctly assessed that I have no *carpentree* DNA. This probably explains why, on the odd occasion when I pick up a hammer or other tool, ostensibly to try to fix something, my family members' instincts to find a safe area well away from whatever it is that I'm intending to rectify are well justified.

While on the subject of timber, a very similar yet seldom-used word these days may cast light on how humans learned to speak. Phonetically pronounced the same as timber, is the word timbre, which means 'the character or quality of a musical sound or voice, distinct from its pitch and intensity.' Is this wording similarity just a logical outcome of comparing the qualities of timber to the qualities of sound in the human voice? Or could it be another reminder of the subtle forces of our tree ancestors leaving traces for us to remember our roots?

'Going against the grain' is an expression that derives from the physical act of rubbing a hand against the grain of a piece of timber, which will likely result in splinters. The expression has taken on the meaning of doing or saying something that is contrary to our natural inclination or conscience. Although it is logical that this wording should arise from working with wood, it is possible that it is our ancestors' way of passing on moral guidelines. Then again, it may simply be their way of showing extreme displeasure at having been cut down. After all, a splinter is a felled tree's last chance to inflict revenge.

'Crawling out of the woodwork' is an old expression referring to ants or bugs infesting timber. The term was coined in olden days when most dwellings were made from wood, and bugs literally crawled out of the woodwork looking for a safe refuge after the timber was moved or damaged for some reason. These days, the term has taken on a human aspect and is used sometimes in relation to many people wanting to express an opinion or take advantage of someone or some situation. For example, when someone wins the lottery, all sorts of people 'come out of the woodwork' with their hands outstretched for a loan they never intend to repay. Perhaps, as with the splinter being a tree's last chance to inflict revenge, this is also a way in which our ancestors showed their displeasure at being hewn down.

The most likely term that relates us to our ancestors is 'knock on wood', also expressed as 'touch wood'. In many cultures, it is common for superstitious people to knock their knuckles on a wooden object to either bring good fortune or ward off bad luck. The phrase can be traced to the 19th century, but its origins are debatable. The most likely explanation relates it to ancient Celtic cultures, whose pagan beliefs embraced spirits and gods thought to reside in trees. Knocking on tree trunks was a way to rouse the tree spirits so they could be called on for protection or to express gratitude for a stroke of good luck. Christians have been known to embrace the practice in relation to the wood of the cross from Christ's crucifixion. Personally, I have occasionally observed someone use the expression, then tap their head in the absence of any wood immediately to hand. A silent, subliminal act precipitated perhaps by deeply rooted ancient connections?

On a slightly different tack from tree-related words are the many references relating to humans that come from our association with birds. From previous chapters showing how closely we are related to birds and the probability they are also tree descendants I consider the following examples are valid associations with our feathered cousins. Depending on our sleep patterns, we label ourselves as either owls or larks. In physical appearance, we can be swans or ugly ducklings. In behaviour, we can be good eggs or bad eggs. We can be as proud as peacocks, naked as jaybirds, sitting ducks or off on a wild goose chase. We can be lovebirds, stool pigeons, empty nesters, spring chickens (or no spring chicken), rare birds, odd birds or completely cuckoo. More sombrely, we can be as dead as a dodo.

My final and most significant entry for this chapter focusses on the word 'sap'. Just as blood is essential for human life, the same applies to sap for the life of a tree. The dictionary meaning for the word is 'the fluid which circulates in the vascular system of a plant, consisting chiefly of water with dissolved sugars and mineral salts.' From sap comes the word 'sapping', defined as 'to gradually weaken or destroy (a person's strength or power), to gradually diminish the supply or intensity of …' Why would a word defining the loss of vital life fluid from a tree be used in the same context as the loss of blood in humans, unless it has been ordained in some way by trees themselves?

THE THEORY OF TREEVOLUTION AND THE FUTURE

𝆃𝆄𝆅

I n a perfect world, if the ideas and suggestions outlined and discussed in the previous chapters come to be accepted, the following scenarios give a glimpse of how I see the impact of Treevolution playing out throughout the world over the next 10–20 years.

Medicine

Medical companies will re-embrace nature, producing therapies and vaccines to help bring peoples' lives back into balance by negating bad influences from their ancestral backgrounds and introducing positive influences. For example, imagine what profound effects and benefits on so many people and society in general, would be seen from a treatment to overcome the effects of addiction from being cursed with excessive *lottree* DNA. Antidotes or vaccines will be developed to prevent or *treet* epidermodysplasia verruciformis, lipoedema, dendrophilia and possibly, spontaneous human combustion. Medical schools will spend far more time training doctors on the therapeutic properties of plant and tree derivatives to prevent and heal many common conditions. There are seeds of hope here.

Barely a week passes when there isn't a report in the media on the results of a study on a plant, espousing its positive benefits for human health. Inevitably though, just as a cow pat attracts bushflies, such announcements are soon followed up with dire warnings from those who oversee our health systems. They talk about the dangers inherent in the safety, unknown side effects, consequences of taking unregulated substances and so on, with the inevitable final statement being to 'always consult your doctor before taking unprescribed substances'. Pragmatic though this advice may be, I can't help but feel it is often a convenient statement designed to shut down the prospects of a potentially beneficial substance from nature making inroads to the profits of large pharmaceutical companies. The latest and most prominent example of the above jostling for control in the medical arena has been the push to legalise medicinal cannabis. One cannot blame doctors here. Faced with a patient brandishing the latest findings on the next great panacea for their health issue, and in all probability knowing little to nothing about it, what doctor is going to take on the obvious risks and sanction its use?

In Australia, I foresee medical students spending less time studying in sterile surroundings, instead being out in the forests, national parks and the outback with First Australian healers, learning the secrets of plants gleaned from 60,000 years of experience. Educational facilities will be appropriately designed with biophilic architectural principles to blend in with the environment and be sited within or close to forests and other identified regions to accommodate the new studies arising from treevolution.

Lastly, and most importantly, will be the development of the special medical facilities needed to provide the diagnostic processes and administer the custom-blended elixirs to balance diagnosed personality and character traits, as agreed to by the individual and the medical specialists. New, purpose-built facilities will also be constructed to produce the relevant tree extracts. These will most likely be located within or near the forests that will contain trees grown in proportion to the demand for their particular extracts. Whether the management and ownership of all these forests, extract production, diagnostic and administration facilities will be government-controlled or left to private enterprises remains to be seen. If it is left to the latter, I foresee many private investors potentially making a lot of money by investing in these ventures. Hopefully, so will thousands of ordinary working Australians benefit financially through earnings of such enterprises feeding back into their superannuation funds. Irrespective of how this pans out, the initial need for workers to build the facilities, and then the numbers of scientists, retrained medical professionals, students, plantation workers, transport drivers and administration personnel will be a boon to the economic growth of regional areas. Having spent much of my working life calling on pharmacies in a retail capacity, I hope they are one currently operating business model that benefits from all this. Besides, who else could be more naturally qualified to dispense these new products than those who are descendants of *chemistrees*. Medical researchers will be falling over themselves to glean the secrets to the long lives of some tree species to be the first to patent an elixir to healthy longevity.

Aside from these more industrial developments, I foresee the Japanese practice of shinrin-yoku becoming more widespread, with its positive benefits being recognised to the extent that many health benefits funds will pay rebates for participating fund members. Along with blood type, people will also have their tree DNA profile uploaded to their medical health record. With regard to overall health, it will become common knowledge that if one is feeling a bit down or depressed, a trip to the countree will help improve the spirits. Having read this far, it should now be clear as to why this would be. General health hints from doctors and health funds will promote this message, with the added recommendation (or prescription) to hug a tree or two, daily.

Science

A whole new branch of science will be needed to study the links between trees and humans. An ideal outcome will be when all trees with specific knowledge and wisdom can be identified and documented and then able to be matched with their human descendant. This will aid the overseers of various tree farms in determining how many of each tree type to propagate depending on commercial demands for preparations of extracts for elixirs, medicines and so on.

The study of trees and their human links will be a new field necessitating the expertise of anthropologists and zooarchaeologists. A specialist field will study the relationships between human fingerprints and tree rings, while etymologists will look into the link between 'tree' words and the originating tree type. Specialised science facilities will analyse tree extracts of sap, syrup and resins to develop the preparations for medical prescriptions used to treat the wide range of conditions outlined in this work.

Assisted reproduction

One of the great challenges facing some couples is the desire to have children, yet for physiological reasons, some have difficulty fulfilling this desire. Many turn to various fertility facilities. Many are successful, but many others are not. The emotional and physical strains on those involved, exacerbated by the financial costs, are considerable. Perhaps research into peoples' tree *ancestree* may alert couples to the potential challenges they may face before finding out the hard way that the journey to parenthood may not be smooth sailing. I envisage the spawning of allied enterprises similar to organisations such as Ancestry.com, which may be able to provide a similar chart showing an individual's tree *ancestrees*. This information may be able to calculate the probability of success in reproduction for the couple involved. I would hope that any such organisations would be allied to reputable hospital and/or medical operations, rather than left to private enterprise, where lack of controls will inevitably lead to charlatan opportunists taking advantage of human vulnerability.

Paediatricians

This branch of childhood health will flourish thanks to new plant-based elixirs and extracts, particularly applicable in the early years of childhood.

Most parents are aware of the stresses a two-year-old child can inflict. Their cute, adorable, cuddly baby suddenly morphs into a lifeform that is seemingly intent on destroying the ones it needs for its own survival, which does not seem to be a smart strategy for any species of living entity wanting to prolong its own longevity. I suggest what happens to toddlers is an internal fight between the different ancestral tree natures, which usually sorts itself out after about a year. Once that period is over, the small human evolves to display all its unique characteristics in a more civilised manner. Family life can then be a wonderful ride until the next battle of the tree species erupts in the early teenage years. If these periods of turmoil can be mitigated to a large degree by understanding and then balancing internal influences, life may be so much better for everyone.

Hair loss

With reference to my earlier and somewhat lengthy discourse on hair loss under *hereditrees*, some enterprising scientific-based company will surely pinpoint the processes by which evergreen trees hold on to their foliage. Consequently, by isolating the gene and patenting it, they will be able to make a tablet or vaccine that will help millions of men and women return their thinning pate back to its former glory. More importantly, it should also help those whose excessive levels of deciduous tree DNA results in them having the more serious condition, alopecia areata. At present, there is no cure for this condition, but the fact that it commonly runs in families is an encouraging sign that a rebalancing of DNA with evergreen species will most likely lead to a long-term solution for future generations.

Plastic surgery

With the advances in medicine that will include behavioural and psychological tree DNA balancing genes to enable humans to feel better about themselves, there will be a dramatic drop in cosmetic surgery procedures. Less botoxed, wasp-lipped, frozen-faced, unhappy ventriloquist people and fewer unscrupulous, unqualified opportunists preying on peoples' emotions (not to mention their wallets) can only be a good thing.

Psychiatree

Psychiatrists face a 'there is the good news and the bad news' situation. The good news is that those who have high levels of the *psychiatree* tree gene are likely to be happier and more successful in their careers. The qualifications they proudly hang on their office walls will certify their psychiatric suitability, no doubt with their credentials having been written over a background of their proud ancestral *psychiatree*, thereby giving them an added status and seal of credibility. These people will be in high demand and in a position to charge appropriately and it would not surprise me to read at some stage that psychiatrists regularly earn more in a year than lawyers! University aspirants for this profession will be chosen based on their *psychiatree* tree DNA levels. Ultimately, this can only be a good thing as the quality of help provided to clients should be expected to improve. The not-so-good news is that some of those currently in the profession may not have much, if any, *psychiatree* DNA, resulting in a lack of credibility and corresponding decline in clients and income. They may then need the services of one of their appropriately endorsed peers. Generally, there will be a gradual decline in the numbers of psychiatrists, as the twin benefits of people spending more time interacting with nature outdoors and having appropriate tree gene antidotes to negate negative ancestral traits will reduce the need for their services.

Mental Health

Mental health is a burgeoning issue of great concern. To me it is no wonder. There has been so much change to the way we live and think over the past 50 years that the poor brain is struggling to make sense of it all. As one of the lucky humans collectively referred to as baby boomers, I have the great advantage of having grown up in a time when life was simpler and much less stressful than today. Technology during the post war years of the 50s, 60s, 70s and 80s consisted of electricity in the home, a black bakelite dial phone on the wall, a black and white television, and maybe a family car. As a young male growing up in Australia, if you had a second-hand bicycle, owned a wristwatch by the age of 18 and had a leather wallet with a few dollars in it, life was good.

The ever-advancing developments in technology, inextricably intertwined with the creeping pressure of consumerism over the years, now has an 18-year-old of either sex effectively welded to a mobile phone 24 hours a day, where they can be exposed to all manner of communication, much of which is not beneficial to their health of mind. Families had to bear the cost of a phone rental (if they had a phone at all) in those early years, but in today's world, that same family now has to fund a mobile phone for each member, the cost of each phone's connection, subscriptions costs for apps and streaming services, internet connection costs, home computers, laptops or tablets and colour printers that voraciously consume replaceable ink cartridges. This is not to say these changes do not have benefits. They obviously can contribute greatly to our lives, but there are associated pressures that are unavoidable, especially to one's finances and mental health.

I do not claim to be an expert in this area, but there are two pieces of advice I would offer to anyone dealing with the pressures of life. The first is to get out into nature as often as possible – our physical wellbeing and our souls are wired for this. The second is to spend less time worrying about your own issues, real or perceived, and do something for someone else. I suggest volunteering for any organisation that helps others or focuses on environmental or wildlife issues.

Euthanasia

A new generation of funeral businesses will spring up, offering various sanctioned options for departing this world, with sensible safeguards in place to minimise fraudulent homicides. While most states in Australia have finally introduced laws enabling voluntary assisted dying, I, like many others, believe they are too restrictive. Personally, just as I have a note on my driving licence identifying me as an organ donor should I meet some tragic end, I would like to have the addition of a euthanasia symbol. This would alert those who need to know, that I have previously set down criteria for the end of my life in what is known as an 'Advanced Care Directive.' This document states my preferred parameters for medical treatment should I become incapable of managing my own affairs, with the additional directive outlining the parameters of my wishes for my life to end, without the bureaucratic red tape and hurdles currently imposed.

Many of these new enterprises will be affiliated with tree *cemetrees*, which are mentioned in more detail in the next section. Some people may prefer to have their ashes mixed with the soil their tree is planted into, while others will opt for biodegradable shrouds, so that their tree can be planted directly over them. For the latter option, people may want this to occur immediately after they are euthanised.

These last options cannot occur in Australia until we are rid of those elected members of parliament who appear to be a century or two out of touch with the realities, needs and wants of the many more enlightened individuals living in our modern world. I suspect some of these people still secretly hold the notion that the earth is flat and steadfastly cling to old ideology in continuing to deny the wishes of most of the people who elected them. Still, money is a powerful catalyst for changing government ministers' minds. Given that they are constantly trying to find savings in their budgets, I feel that once they realize that if each of the 2.5 million Australians currently receiving the aged or service pension were to depart the world an average of just one week earlier than would otherwise be the case, it would save them $1.25 billion over the combined period of their lives (based on a conservative average weekly pension amount of $500). Now, I am no expert, but I feel certain that savings of this magnitude would be more than adequate to cover the costs of setting up the facilities, legalities and procedures to ensure due process is observed. Just as people who choose to have an imprint on their driver's licence that confirms they are 'organ donors', so too will those who have made plans to be euthanised be afforded the choice of a similar suitable imprint.

Tree cemetrees

Here is a wonderful opportunity for enterprising funeral businesses to make some ground-breaking changes to the current options available to their clients. Soon, options will be available for tree burials in beautiful forests reserved for such purposes. Ideally, some of these tree *cemetrees* could be incorporated into those forests planted as natural fire breaks.

Again, a project of this size will create employment for many whose previous occupations have dwindled or disappeared through the restructuring needed to save our world. Families will be able to visit their dearly departed and instead of looking at words etched into a cold, stark, granite headstone, they will be able to see them as living, thriving trees, suitably selected from related ancestral species. Due to the area needed between each tree to allow them to grow to their full maturity, there will be ample space for families to set up tables and celebrate family milestones in the shade of their memory, with the peace, respect and family bonding that such a setting would naturally bring. Future generations will be encouraged to take seeds or fruit from a family member's tree and further the legacy of their loved one by planting them elsewhere.

This concept first came to me so many years ago that I cannot remember exactly when. However, I know it was triggered by the memory of seeing trees lining the road into Ballarat in Victoria. The Ballarat Avenue of Honour holds 3,801 trees from 23 different species of mostly European deciduous origins (including ash, oak, maple, alder, birch, elm, lime and poplars) that were planted in memory of men and women from the town and district who enlisted in the Australian Imperial Forces during World War I. At 22 km long, it is the longest planting of its kind in Australia. In all, there were 121 listed Avenues of Honour planted during this period, 92 of which are in Victoria. They are such a wonderful commemorative legacy that brings a living, breathing individuality of the memory of those who served. Perhaps this concept could be reintroduced for non-military civilians in towns, with family members contributing to the care and maintenance of their tree and a small commemorative plaque, just as is currently the case with many privately funded memorial bench seats in peaceful spots all across the country.

Religion

It is difficult to predict what effects treevolution will have on world religions. It is unlikely it will have an impact on the major religions other than Christianity in English speaking *countrees*. I state this as I believe it would be highly unrealistic and egotistical of me to suggest that this work will be translated into other languages in the first place. Secondly, even if it was translated and widely read, my perspective on other world religions suggests that, in most instances, treevolution would align with many other belief systems.

The biggest opportunity for change may come from within Christianity, because we know that with each census taken (certainly in Australia), more people are indicating that they have no religion. Given the internal troubles embroiling the church due to the surfacing of the depraved sexual acts perpetrated by high office leaders, I suspect that this movement away from Christianity will continue. It would not surprise me to see a jump in the numbers looking to the past to embrace one of the oldest marginalised world religions, paganism. Founded on ancient spiritual traditions based on a reverence for nature, with particular beliefs that spirits reside within trees, this religion has a natural affinity with treevolution. It is here that those who feel the need for spiritual fulfilment are likely to find a home.

Realistically, it may be time for the leaders of all the different religions to meet and form a new-world spiritual ideology. This could morph the accepted, time-proven principles of each into a universal code of conduct focussed on bringing out the best in humanity in today's world, unfettered from the shackles of outdated scripture. I suspect this may be a long time coming. Still, I am not alone in this view. The English writer and speaker, Christopher Hitchens, well-known for his views on world religions, wrote the following in 'God Is Not Great':

> *Above all, we are in need of a renewed Enlightenment, which will base itself on the proposition that the proper study of mankind is man and woman.*[19]

Astrology

Many people are besotted with astrology and take the birthdates and star signs of potential partners very seriously. I admit to being somewhat of a sceptic in this area, although I must admit that from my limited experience, the characteristics of the natures of the different star signs do appear to have a fair degree of synergy with treevolution. I was interested to see if there were any consistent correlations between the character attributes of various star signs and an individual's tree profiling, so it was only natural that I compared my Libran character

19 Christopher Hitchens (2008, p. 283). *God is not Great: How Religion Poisons Everything.* Atlantic Books

traits with those of my tree heritage profile outlined at the end of the chapter, The I to Z of Tree Words.

The first challenge in attempting this was the many varied and subtle differences between various astrologers. I eventually settled on selecting those attributes common to most of the astrology profiles I looked at. These included reference to Librans looking to keep a balanced aspect in all situations, seeking justice and quality, always trying to be objective, and always doing what is in the best interest of everyone. From my perspective, I consider this pretty accurate, but I dare say these qualities could well apply to most other star signs as well. Lacking in the above rosy description is a Libran's inability to make quick decisions, or for that matter, any decision. The outcome of this is that the correlations between the two assessments are reasonably close, but not as clearly defined as I had hoped for. I confess to preferring the astrological Libran depiction to my treevolutionary self-appraisal. Perhaps I am being too hard on myself. Obviously, plenty of work could be done in analysing astrological and treevolutionary traits, perhaps in a sequel to this work.

Palmistree

Practitioners in this field will experience a rapid increase in demand for their services. Experienced exponents of this art will be sought to train the growing numbers of new devotees and demand from dating sites, company human resource managers and services such as Ancestry. com. I must find an experienced practitioner for myself before this boom. Perhaps they could dispel my sense of scepticism. I might try tricking them by pointing to the lines that I have accumulated through various unintended means over my life and asking them what they mean. If they identify that they are lines from accidents or self-inflicted stupidity without hesitation, I think I could be a convert. Whether or not these exponents tap into my theories linking fingerprints to tree types remains to be seen, but it would certainly be an opportunity to add credibility to their art.

Finding true love

At present, dating sites use information provided mainly by the applicants. This can easily be manipulated to present a profile that may be quite different from the truth. Through the addition of an applicant's tree DNA profile, businesses providing this service can check for legitimate information, weed out fraudsters and allow for minor amendments, thereby giving greater security to both the romantic hopefuls and the owners of dating sites. Most importantly, the odds of finding that special someone will be greatly improved. The general rule of opposites attracting is still a good rule-of-thumb. For example, one partner is usually better at handling finances than the other in most relationships. Imagine for a moment, two people together with high levels of *budgetree* DNA. They may end up rich but have a less-than-happy life because they were always focussed on saving and not spending to enjoy it. On the other hand, two people with high *lottree* DNA may be headed for poverty or bankruptcy, unless of course they do win the *lottree* – although how often do we hear of winners of large sums of money who end up blowing the lot in a short period of time anyway, losing friends and family in the process? As we have seen from earlier examples, the powers of our ancestral tree DNA mould our character and direct our actions.

Family planning

Notwithstanding any health issues, if a couple has well-balanced tree genes, nature will take care of the rest. I predict that within the next two generations the name 'Forest' will rise worldwide to be ranked in the top ten names throughout English-speaking *countrees* and be the top chosen name for boys from now on. It sounds great and every time they hear their name called, they will be reminded of their past and how great they can be, so why not? As discussed previously, understanding a person's tree origins is going to play a major role in companies offering assisted reproduction services, resulting in faster, more effective and more affordable outcomes which will reduce the emotional and financial stresses on clients.

Sex

I have no doubt that the scramble to be the first enterprise to successfully patent a safe and easy-to-use tree extract to help men suffering with erectile dysfunction in silence the world over, will be intense. The most likely source for this will undoubtedly be obtained from one of the hardwood species!

The economy

Governments the world over will quickly realise the benefits arising from treevolution, from the growth in new enterprises and the taxes this will bring, and in huge pension cost savings from euthanasia options as discussed earlier in this chapter. Humans who lose their way in life, from convicted criminals to lonely souls who feel that life is pointless, will find new purpose and drive by visiting specialised clinics that will balance out and realign their damaging attitudes and behaviours. This will enable these people to ease back into the work world, thereby easing the financial burden on government social security payments. Just as we have rehab clinics to treat drug, alcohol, gambling, sex and other addictions, there will be an explosion of life clinics, which will be run by qualified medical professionals trained in the preparation of potions with ingredients from specific tree types to correct identified character imbalances. The financial savings of reducing recidivist offending from reformed criminals alone will reduce costs on our prison systems as well as crime levels and at the same time, put downward pressure on insurance premiums. The drain on the economy to fund unemployment benefits will steadily reduce and people will flock to volunteer their time and skills to countless organisations that desperately need additional help. Subsequently, this will lead people back into the states of mind and health that increase their chances of finding paid employment.

Capitalism: Governments and economies

I would like to think it is abundantly clear to anyone with half a brain that our current economic system of growth and expansion is absurdly unsustainable. This is because it is largely fuelled by more debt to fund more production, to make more stuff for more people to create more waste and pollution to hasten the point at which civilization as we know it will collapse under the weight of its own excreta. At the time I wrote those words, towards the end of July 2020, in relative sanctuary from the health impacts of COVID-19 by virtue of living in Adelaide, I had an uneasy feeling that capitalism as we know it may be headed towards a major collapse. I thought it would require some type of life support while the world leaders modified or created a completely new financial system. Interest rates were at historical lows and government borrowing soared to help stem the impacts of the coronavirus pandemic on businesses and citizens' livelihoods. What would happen if the world of commerce did not make a full and speedy recovery? How would governments pay back this mounting debt when millions of its former taxpaying citizens were looking down a long dark tunnel, wondering not when, but if, they would get back to working and earning an amount near their previous income? Through job losses and lockdowns, what would happen if sufficient numbers of people, especially the young, lost heart and stopped buying into the dream of home ownership and all the material stuff that goes with it? What would happen if it all became unattainable, causing people to readjust their thinking about life priorities and realising that the endless pursuit of material goods to signify success is just not worth the effort? It was possible that sufficient numbers of people were already on the cusp of a cultural shift and a change in our value systems. People were beginning to think that less is more and prefer quality over quantity. Such a shift could be disastrous for economies built on credit and consumerism, but a boon to the opportunities outlined in this book.

Business

Apart from the boon to ventures such as dating and heritage sites, there will be growth in the health drinks industry. Sap smoothies will be the new go-to health-fix. Resin-based beers will be the go-to drink for deciduous descendants clutching at every opportunity to protect their crowning glory. Shampoo and conditioner manufacturers' sales will go through the roof with the new line of offerings containing sap and resin. Massage and spa centres will offer clients a choice of tree sap and resin oils as part of the service to improve the effects of their *treetments*.

Human resources departments in large businesses will utilise the benefits of tree profiling in better matching potential job aspirants to available positions within the organisation.

Sales Training

I learned a long time ago that, in our western world at least, 'nothing happens until someone sells something.' Whether that happens to be in a traditional salesperson-customer situation, a teacher trying to impart knowledge to their students, a priest delivering a sermon to his flock, or a frustrated mother trying to get her two-year old to understand that it is not okay to begin their artistic career by smearing the walls of the house with their excrement, it's a pretty apt statement. Of the many sales courses I attended over my career, one of the most useful was one based on the Myers-Briggs personality profiling. Based on Carl Jung's theory of psychological personality types, this program asserts there are four dimensions to our personality preferences. These are: where we focus our attention, the way we process information, the way we make decisions and how we generally relate to the world. I have no doubt that the sixteen different personality types they have identified could be matched to their relevant trees, particularly to the emotional and character tree words ending in 'ty'.

I would love to give some examples, but I'm sure I would be in danger of breaching various commercial laws if I did. All I can confirm is that I went through this exercise knowing my Myers-Briggs personality profile and matched it with my self-assessed tree profile and the compatibility was pretty accurate. The point is, treevolution will become an added tool in helping sales businesses select candidates for careers based on their genetic predispositions. Needless to say, for the same reasons, employment agencies will also be in a far better situation to match their clients with careers.

Technology

Over the past fifty years, we have had to adapt to the development of transformational new technologies – including the personal computer, the World Wide Web, the internet, mobile communications, virtual reality, robotics and artificial intelligence – all designed with the intention of benefiting and advancing our lives. But for all this technology, there are at least two big questions that need to be answered. Has all this technology made us smarter and are we better human beings because of it? Have we become more self-aware, kinder, understanding and compassionate? Have our behaviours, cultures and leadership advanced?

Technology cannot solve moral problems. I think many people, particularly those like me who remember a world without all this technology, feel as though they are drifting uncontrollably toward a world that we don't quite understand, nor really want, but feel helpless to stop it or slow it down. It seems the digital revolution that has the potential to enrich our lives may actually be compounding today's widening economic inequality, unemployment rates and cultural divides. Today's digital economy is characterised by an uncontrolled free market, corporate irresponsibility, privacy issues and a proliferation of sites infested with online scammers. In addition to this, there has been a proliferation of online games and gambling sites developed to hook people with addictive natures, along with an infestation of violent content. This all shows an alarming widescale ignorance of this technology's impact on our social, mental and physical wellbeing, especially for young people. And this is all before we get to the 'dark web', which is infested with drug and arms dealers, paedophiles, and other criminals. When we consider all these elements together, we have a communications system functioning in ways far from the altruistic aims of its developers.

Andrew Keen, in his fourth book, *How to Fix the Future – Staying Human in the Digital Age*,[20] alerts us to the stark reality that our technology might be developing a mind of its own. He surmises that the existential threat of 'self-conscious' computer algorithms developing minds of

---

20 Andrew Keen (2018). *How to Fix the Future – Staying human in the digital age*. Atlantic Books.

their own with the potential to exclude, disempower and enslave us, is very real. When he states that the world's richest man, Bill Gates, and the world's most famous physicist, the late Stephen Hawking, and many other prominent men have also shared these concerns, there is good cause to be alarmed. Stanley Kubrick's 1968 film, *2001: A Space Odyssey*, no longer seems so futuristic. Keen references two studies in his book. One forecasts potential job losses of up to 47% over the next twenty years through the influence of smart technology. The other predicts that 49% of current working time could be automated by current technology. Human *histree* has a way of repeating itself, largely due to the *predatree* natures that continually draw us into conflict with our fellow beings, but also because we do not learn the lessons of the past. Keen surmises that the current status of power, control and wealth held by the digital monopolies is drawing us to a point where we are on the edge of following the fallout that happened during the industrial age of the early to mid-eighteenth century. This period saw the wealth and power residing with the few, and millions effectively enslaved in poverty. If these forecasts and predictions come anywhere near to playing out, how will humans adapt to such dramatic change over such a relatively short period of time? Especially those who have only ever lived in a digital world.

There are two key positive effects the lessons from treevolution can have on mitigating the dangers posed by these threats. The first is the impact on job creation. Whether it is through the economic fallout precipitated by the coronavirus pandemic, the effects of job losses through automation or a combination of both, the new opportunities outlined in this chapter – while not a complete solution – will surely provide a solid platform for job creation. The second positive effect will be the psychological and physiological benefits that will arise from working in the environments where these new industries will be centred – principally forests, national parks and other natural regions decentralised from major urban hubs. It is here that the environmental, scientific and technological worlds can be fused into a harmonious relationship that will make us healthier, smarter, wiser and kinder humans. Before this can happen, the unfettered expansion of digital technology and those propelling it need to be held accountable. This will never happen with so-called industry regulation. According to Keen, the necessary changes will only come about from a combination of government regulation, competitive innovation, social responsibility, worker and consumer choice, and education. While I support his summation, I would add that the overriding proviso must be that the needs of our environment and Mother Nature should be foremost in thought, planning and implementation.

Education

There is a growing awareness of the number of children experiencing stress and anxiety at younger and younger ages. A program called Nurturing Nature was created in Scotland in 2009.[21] The program aimed to see what changes would occur in young children's responses to stress and fear responses caused by abuse and trauma when they interacted within natural environments. The children were given structured, supervised time outdoors to climb trees, roll down hills, interact with farm animals, pick fruit and vegetables, and collect wood for campfires. The positive results included increased resilience, enhanced social and emotional strengths and improvements in self-regulation and initiative. The program is gradually being adopted, albeit slowly, through other learning facilities for children. I find it both absolutely bizarre and ironic that, in the space of 60 years, we have lost what kids of my generation did naturally and took for granted. Perhaps it is best to have the adult supervision, though I have no regrets about having had what I see now was the simple luxury in my youth of doing all those things and much more. Naturally, there was also the added dimension of excitement, exhilaration and moments of fear that came when obtaining fruit and vegetables in ways that would probably not be acceptable now. Only 200 years ago, those escapades would have seen me exiled to a life of penal servitude and suffering in a far off *countree*! I can only imagine what dilemmas and opportunities this work affords specialist fields such as sociology and anthropology.

---

21 Learning through Landscapes. *Nurturing Nature*. ltl.org.uk/projects/nurturing-nature/

In his book *Blinded by Science*,[22] Matthew Silverstone reveals scientific data showing that trees improve many health issues, particularly the mental conditions, ADHD and depression. Trees can also relieve headaches and improve reaction times and concentration. He lists many studies of children who showed significant psychological and physiological improvements in their health and wellbeing when they interacted with trees and plants. He reasons that everything in nature vibrates, and different vibrations affect biological behaviour, with trees being able to bring the human body into a healing alignment. Now if that is not a strong supporting statement for my theory, I don't know what is! Just as trees absorb carbon to cleanse the air, they can facilitate the cleansing and revitalising of all the stored up negative energy and stress humans experience. Being in the presence of trees realigns our vibrations with their healthy and grounding ones. How can this be if we are not in some way connected with them? The deep emotions involved in this level of connectedness are driven by a primitive, subconscious understanding that our roots are very much interconnected with those of our tree ancestors.

With this rediscovery of the powerful effects that trees have on us, schools will develop outdoor areas where trees are the focal point. When weather conditions are suitable, these areas will be used as study zones for relevant subjects that require inspiration, imagination and creativity. Dendrology (the science and study of wooded plants) will become a *mandatree* subject at high schools. Further, all high school graduates will have a complete understanding of their tree *ancestree* and the influence this will have on the key areas of their lives – health, vocational direction, *monetree* management and relationships. Many of the medical practitioners of the future will come through *elementree* schools, where the curriculum focus 'tree' component of the word elementary will start at a young age.

---

22 Matthew Silverstone. *Blinded by Science*. www.blindedbyscience.co.uk/

The English language

Just what affect this work will have on the English language will be interesting to see. Whether the original spelling of the 'tree' words will be reinstated or not is something for the academics to work through, hopefully with guidance and wisdom from selected ancestral trees. I am sure there will be much lively debate. Irrespective of this, my main hope is that our language is not decimated by the political correctness mentality eating into it. Who knows, men may even find their collective voice and rise up (in a peaceable way of course) to prevent mangoes from being renamed womgoes or femgoes, or some wishy-washy inoffensive name like sunset fruit or happy peaches! No doubt there will be changes to the current meanings of certain words and phrases. As an example, I can see that in future, referring to someone as a birdbrain will mean they are intellectually somewhere on the spectrum between nerdy and genius. Similarly, many other words will be replaced or reassigned to more accurately reflect the meaning our ancestors intended.

The English monarchy

The widespread acceptance of treevolution will enhance the relevance and standing of the Royal Family. With new-found respect, King Charles will personally bestow knighthoods on those who have the vision, courage and tenacity to bring about the changes needed to reverse our lemming mentality of expansion and consumerism. Business leaders throughout the world will listen to his words on the environment, climate change and the need to rewire our economies for sustainable growth in earnest, rather than through protocol and political correctness pressures. I am sure he would also enjoy presenting wooden medals to the victors at Commonwealth Games events. Hopefully, Prince William will continue his work. In 2020, the Prince of Wales launched The Earthshot Prize, designed to find, encourage and reward climate innovators who are tackling the greatest existential threats to our planet. Hopefully, his younger brother, Prince Harry, does not allow the strong influences of *derogatrees, condemnatrees* and *inflammatrees* to derail his past efforts to the same ends.

Cultural change

One of the biggest challenges we face is how best to deal with the continuous pressure to buy and accumulate 'stuff'. Most of us would have seen one of those television programs that feature people who have become hoarders and are barely able to move around the piles of material built up in their own homes over years of collecting. While these are the extreme examples of drowning in clutter, most of us are more likely to be nearer to this situation than the few who could claim to be minimalists in material possessions, not through poverty but by choice.

One suggestion to help break this cycle for our children is in regard to birthdays. We have become so indoctrinated with materialism that it is just unthinkable to attend a child's birthday party without bringing an appropriately wrapped gift. Many parents with school-aged children are buckling under the financial pressures this imposes and the requirement to store the stuff their own children get when they have a party. With a shift in attitudes, instead of wrapped 'stuff' being given, perhaps the invitations could request a small donation (maximum $10.00 as a suggestion) to cover the purchase of a plant or small tree. Then, all party invitees can travel to a government- or council-endorsed area where community planting is welcomed. I am sure the many volunteer organisations caring for our environment would be happy to offer experienced people to help with the planting process. As a bonus, children get out in the fresh air, experience nature, and do something worthwhile for the environment. Plus, apart from disposing of the plant containers (which are usually recyclable) no-one is burdened with more stuff. The same process could be adopted by adults, and for occasions other than birthdays. The current celebratory days for mother's, father's, Anzacs, New Year's and even Australia days, could all be commemorated, with special days of remembrance for lost loved ones as well.

Sport

Like trees, the world needs more sport. I do not need to espouse the myriad benefits it brings. The fervour many people have toward their chosen sport borders on religious. In this regard, I have always felt there are similarities between religion and sport. Each sport and each religion developed its own distinct history, culture, rules, legends or deities, clothing and devoted followers. The biggest difference is that any sports lover can get together with someone from a totally different sport and have a chat without getting into a war over whose game is better. This is because they each understand that the reasons for playing or following their respective sport in the first place are essentially the same (curling and synchronised swimming may be the exceptions).

I have often thought that the ongoing problems in the Middle East could be dramatically mitigated if the *countrees* were flushed with water to grow and sustain sporting fields and trees. If the people of these regions played as much sport as Australians do, their minds and hearts would become focussed on more constructive ways of channelling *predatree* aggression. They simply would not have the time or desire to be involved in senseless age-old conflicts. Granted, I dare say there could well be a shortage of referees and umpires in the early days at least, but those willing would be handsomely paid! I can foresee supporters and players of the fiercest of sporting rivals – like soccer icons Liverpool and Manchester United – sharing the same pub venues after a game with no ill feelings (although this may take some time to come to fruition)! The growing sport of tree climbing will become popular to the point where it will replace curling at the Olympic Games in the not-too-distant future. Additionally, the winners of events will be awarded the Wooden Medal in honour of our ancestors, with gold and silver being for second and third and bronze being retained in honour all good folk whom God directed to go forth!

Humanity

Once people have traced their ancestral tree roots and understand how they became what and who they are, they will come to appreciate the significance and importance of our roles as custodians in protecting, preserving and caring for Earth's flora and fauna. As we come to realize how we are all connected through our common *ancestree*, one of the greatest flaws in human nature worldwide will fade away. I refer here to racism. When we begin to learn and understand the laws, rituals, beliefs and most importantly, the wisdom sustaining those still-existing ancient cultures, we will start the journey back towards a more harmonious balance with nature and our fellow human beings. Every person on the planet will be educated to reduce their imprint on the earth, with the primary aim being to achieve a carbon-neutral impact over their lifetime. This means reducing waste, recycling and planting – or at least attending to plants and trees – in nurseries, forests and gardens.

In today's world, there is much focus on the latest electronic gadget, fashion, gossip, reality show, sporting result or space discovery. While I can see the merits of sport and space exploration, I feel we have so much more to learn from looking backwards to explore our beginnings in a new light. How wonderful will it be when we can track down our ancestral tree lineage through websites such as Ancestree.com? With a surname like mine, I hope to be able to track right back through the *histree* of animal stags to perhaps an ancient staghorn tree. Maybe there is some truth to the story I used to tell youngsters about the Christmas Eve long ago, when some of Santa's reindeer were sick and a few of my relative stags had to fill in to pull the sleigh. Who knows, I may even be descended from a Rudolph, Dancer, Prancer, Donna or Blitzen! I do like Christmas. Okay, I am probably going a bit too far with this, but you never know!

Histree

Since my diatribe on this word earlier, my thoughts have mellowed somewhat over the writing of this theory. My passionate stance on retaining the status quo with the word history has possibly blinded me to two likely origins for its current spelling and meaning.

Firstly, if we look at the word in light of my theory, it literally translates to mean 'his tree', which was most likely a possessive term, referring to the ownership of a female tree or trees. At the turn of the 19th century, women the world over had few, if any, legal rights. Upon marriage, women surrendered all ownership of property, money and even the rights to guardianship of their children to their husband. It was not until 1902 that all women in Australia were allowed to vote, 16 years before the same rights were accorded women in Britain and the USA. The subjugation of women by men is an appallingly primitive way of living in today's modern world. In most westernised *countrees*, the laws and attitudes have improved since the days of the suffragettes; however, there is still a long road ahead before most men genuinely accept and *treet* women as equals. Sadly, in other regions of our world, it would seem there has been no progress in regard to women's rights at all.

With the Earth being decimated by pollution that, if left unchecked, will inevitably lead to the extinction of most life forms on the planet, and despite the dire warnings of scientists and countless other credentialled humans, our leaders of Governments and Big Business are still hell-bent on expansionism and growth to fuel economies. It is time the men who control world events realise that no amount of money can compensate for lives lost because our water is toxic and our air unbreathable. It is time women are given the reins to guide humanity. Along with this, a rewording and rephrasing of many English words over time to re-feminise it to some fifty-fifty balance, is as inevitable as it is necessary. I suggest the word manure be retained as a poignant reminder of man's legacy in taking life on earth to the brink of extinction.

The second and most likely origin and meaning for *histree* is this. If we add in just one letter and a space to the spelling of history, we get 'his story'. Given the treatment of women up until relatively recent times in western societies, it is highly likely that most of *histree* has been seen, interpreted and recorded predominantly by men.

Irrespective, even if neither of these two meanings can be validated, it is clear a change to the word history must surely be inevitable. The school subject of *histree*, or *herstree*, will be *mandatree* (or should that be *femdatree*) through primary and secondary schooling.

Law and order

Along with fingerprinting, DNA matching, voice recognition and iris analysis, tree profiling will give our law enforcement agencies another avenue to identify people. Additionally, as part of their sentencing, felons might be referred to specialised clinics to have their ancestral behavioural faults modified with the relevant correctional tree vaccines, eventually enabling them to merge back into society as fully functioning model citizens. Highly *predatree* criminal lawyers will become focussed on truth and justice outcomes, instead of the current 'win at all costs irrespective of guilt' mentality that is so frustrating to the communities they purport to serve, thus restoring public confidence in the judicial process. I hasten to suggest this may be a little unrealistic and take some time.

It would be fair to say that, in many instances where crimes are committed and details are in the public domain, there is often outrage at percieved inadequate sentencing outcomes. Contrasting these situations with punishments meted out some 200 years ago for crimes we would now dismiss as trivial, one might be forgiven for wondering how and why these extremes have occurred. I suggest that one of the key differences may lie in the tree lineages from which our past and present law custodians evolved. It seems apparent to me that judges of yesteryear had much higher levels of *condemnatree* DNA than today's judges. Add in a liberal genetic dose from *bigatrees*, *discriminatrees*, *derogatrees*, *mandatrees*, *minatrees*, *reformatrees* and *purgatrees*, and it's no wonder penalties were harsh. Add in a dollop of *migratree* and it's no surprise many of our human ancestors ended up in Australia! By comparison, today's judges appear to have little of these tree influences and seem to be predominantly from *arbitree, conciliatree, approbatree,* or even *commendatree* species. In the future, sentencing of juvenile offenders will include programs to work with and care for trees matching their *ancestree.* There are literally hundreds of *voluntree* organisations throughout Australia operating under the name 'Friends of …' that focus on all manner of environmental initiatives, especially in national parks. Most of these organisations would embrace giving these young offenders the support they need to find purpose in their lives.

Forestrees

In Australia, many people will likely identify that their tree ancestors predominantly align with European forest species. Consequently, there will be a growing demand for more of these tree species to be planted here. Perhaps the best way to accommodate this would be to plant forests that can act as natural firebreaks and safety areas between the vast areas of Australian bush that are prone to explode into flame in the right conditions. A project of this size will create employment for thousands of people whose previous occupations dwindled or disappeared through the restructuring needed to save our world. An upside to this would be when former office-bound workers discover the joys and benefits of experiencing nature. The roads that run through these forests will provide access to new nature areas, resort retreats, bicycle and walking paths, and tree house getaways – the possibilities are as vast as the imagination. Many people who lose their jobs as a result of the economic changes recommended in this work, will find gainful employment, a new spiritual connection and satisfaction from overseeing the planting of trees alongside these roads.

Native to the Northern Hemisphere, plane trees are the last living species of the Platanaceae family. The London plane hybrid (*Platanus acerifolia*) is particularly tolerant of urban conditions. A 2011 study estimated that every year, trees in greater London remove 850–2,000 tonnes of PM10 pollution particles, which are considered harmful to humans. I expect further forestry research will discover ways to develop new strains of Australian trees that are far more resistant to burning in forest fires. These could be planted between the European forest species and Australian eucalypts to act as an additional fire barrier. Areas will be designated for parents to plant a birth tree for each newborn child. Just as many people have birthstones, these trees will match the predominant characteristics of their parents' genes.

Forestree will become a much more desired professional field, with more specialist universities offering appropriate courses run from suitably designed facilities located within forests. People with common tree ancestors will form groups to sponsor and care for forests of their predecessors. Just as many public walkways and buildings are funded by individuals and families who sponsor a custom-designed brick or paver, thousands of people will sponsor individual forest trees. Once the realisation dawns that a good-sized mature tree produces around 100 kg of oxygen per year and adult humans need about 740 kg of oxygen per year, more people will be moved to plant the seven or eight trees needed to at least replace the oxygen they consume during their lifetime. I would love to see the establishment of a movement called 'The Seven Trees Project', where individuals who plant seven trees to offset their lifetime oxygen intake are rewarded in some way for their contribution to the environment. I imagine the travel *industree* embracing new opportunities to organise bus trips under the 'Seven Trees' banner, taking people on tours to *countree* destinations to plant a tree a day for a week. This would boost regional tourism and is a win for the environment.

The growth of *shinrin-yoku* will bring many people from the cities to spend time in forests and in so doing, will help the economies and population growth of regional areas. National *Forestree* Day will be a national holiday, with nationwide and local community events encouraging families to plant at least one tree at a designated site.

With regard to my love for forests and trees in general, I feel it prudent to state I am not advocating that every tree should be sacrosanct – never to be pruned or cut down. While this may be the case for some species and situations – particularly when a greater understanding of spiritual and other trees we learn to communicate with becomes clear – a degree of pragmatic reality must be retained.

Timber and its by-products will probably always be needed and used by humans, so sustainable *forestree* is the key here. That said, every effort will be made to reduce our reliance on timber, particularly in relation to the building of homes. Steel is a viable alternative for this and is already widely used, although there are environmental considerations to take into account with this option. Materials that can be made from recycled plastics and glass should be adopted in other areas where wood is traditionally used. At an international level, the overriding principle must be to identify and protect at all costs, the trees identified as being 'Mother Trees', the 'mysterious, powerful entities that nurture their kin and sustain the forest'.[23]

There must be a concerted worldwide effort to ban cutting down trees that are identified as being what I call knowledge trees (including most of those tree types in the A to H and I to Z of Tree Words in this theory). If this theory is correct, and most of human advancement is influenced by our tree forebears, then apart from the physiological aspects to human welfare, the random destruction of trees is effectively destroying our source of knowledge and inspiration. So far, we have killed off almost half of the world's trees and so most likely, at least half of the font of wisdom and knowledge that was available to us just a few hundred years ago. This may sound cynical, but I can't help thinking this is becoming evident in the quality of many of our world leaders. Where have all the great statesmen and speakers of the past gone? Why haven't they been reborn in the past 30 to 50 years or so? Could it be too many *oratrees* have been eliminated?

In Australia, I predict a key focus will be on studying, protecting and expanding areas of trees that are not only of cultural and spiritual importance to First Australians, but have also been found to have medical benefits specific to their genetic make-up.

23 Suzanne Simard (2021, back cover). *Finding the Mother Tree: Uncovering the Wisdom and Intelligence of the Forest*. Penguin Books Limited

National parks

Australia is blessed with having many national parks. I am fortunate to live a pleasant 6 km bike ride from the beautiful Belair National Park, situated in the foothills about 13 km south-east of Adelaide. Established in 1891, it is the oldest national park in South Australia, and second oldest in Australia, behind Sydney's Royal National Park. The richness of its colonial *histree* is evidenced by the many and varied old buildings (including a former governor's summer residence), pavilions and European trees planted by our forebears as reminders of their *countrees* of origin. Easily accessible, the sealed roads allow visitors to access much of the park and get close to the many points of interest. Walking and shared use trails abound. There are several beautifully maintained ovals, many modern barbeque facilities and shelters, an adventure playground for kids, some thirty-plus tennis courts and the Adelaide to Melbourne rail line weaving through several tunnels in the upper levels of the park to entice train spotters. For nature lovers, there are waterfalls, lakes, creeks, geological features and myriad flora, including over 55 orchids endemic to the park. Naturally, this park is also home to kangaroos, koalas, emus, many other birds, and the more elusive echidnas and southern brown bandicoots. The park has significant cultural ties with the Kaurna people, whose past is evidenced in certain trees and sites that are best found by joining one of the free guided walks. I have no doubt that all other parks have their unique features, as well as the commonalities with nature I have detailed for the Belair National Park. My point here is this: this beautiful park – once a mecca for thousands who came by train, horse-drawn coach or car on Sundays in days past – is largely unappreciated and under-utilised in today's world. In 2024 an estimated 250,000 people visited the park, which is accessible every day of the year unless closed due to the threat of fires during summer months. That is an average of fewer than 700 people a day in an area that covers over 8 km².

In the future, I see visits to many parks being a *mandatree* part of primary and high school curriculums. On guided walks, students will learn about *histree*, geology, indigenous culture, flora, fauna and the importance of conservation in an environment that nurtures their own health and wellbeing. Weather permitting, overnight excursions will enable study of nocturnal animals. The growth in practices like *shinrin-yoku*, will also bring more groups of people to be guided to suitable sites in parks away from the more frequented areas. With the reawakening and understanding of the need to spend more time reconnecting with nature, I foresee the growth in the numbers of people of all ages switching off their computers and getting out in nature.

During their visits, people may even come to the aid of parks to help deal with a huge problem that is largely unseen to the uninformed park visitor. As beautiful as Belair National Park is, much of this beauty would by now be unseen were it not for a small, dedicated volunteer group – The Friends of Belair National Park. Albeit unintentionally, over the years, the introduction of foreign trees and plants to domestic gardens has resulted in some of these species finding a fertile environment in which to thrive in our national parks. Their rapid proliferation has resulted in the suffocation and choking of the natural vegetation, and along with it, the habitats of native animals and birds. In Belair, olive trees and blackberry have made areas of the park inaccessible. Additionally, English broom, gorse, thistle, South African boneseed and daisy, Rhamnus, sollya (*Billardiera heterophylla*), monadenia (*Disa bracteate*), dog roses and others whose names I cannot pronounce, are intruders that need to be curtailed. Several times a week, committed volunteers meet early in the morning to invest a couple of hours in safely and strategically removing these invaders.

At present, the two biggest challenges to seeing the park free of invasive plants is a lack of volunteer numbers and the restrictions of physical stamina caused by the inevitability of advancing years. I do not know what the average age of current volunteers is, but I think I would be right in stating that it's above my own age – and I'm heading toward 76! Regardless, I consider myself privileged to be one of them. When people begin re-embracing nature at the expense of consumerism, financial pressures will ease, hopefully making a four-day working week a reality. With the extra time, volunteer numbers should increase, as many younger hands help out. If nothing else, the time invested is productive, a good physical workout and beneficial for the soul.

Tree huggers

No longer will genuine tree huggers feel any need to keep their practices secret. Once people adopt the principles of treevolution, I feel certain that more tree hugger clubs and societies will spring up around the world. World tree hugging day will become a much-anticipated annual event. The Guinness Book of Records' longest tree-hug record will be smashed. Before one scoffs at such a suggestion, consider this: certified by the Guinness Book of Records, the largest tree hug consisted of 4,620 people. It was achieved by Asianex News Network Pvt Ltd (India) in Thiruvanantha, Puram, India on 21 March, 2017.[24] The attempt was held on the United Nations 'International Day of Forests' and aimed to promote the importance of trees and forests. The appropriate name for the event was 'My Tree, My Life'. Once people know their tree DNA, they will be driven to take up the practice on a regular basis, whenever they want to. By hugging a tree related to their specific species, people will experience physical, mental and emotional benefits that will be shared and widely discussed. Eventually, society at large will become used to seeing people embracing trees because they will understand and respect what they are doing and why.

One well-known sporting identity from the tennis world who is not afraid what people may think of some of the unusual practices he engages in to be the best tennis player in the world is Novak Djokovic. Among his many achievements, he has won 10 Australian Men's Singles tennis titles, four more than the next best on that list. For the past 16 years, on his quests to win these tournaments, he visited and spent time with a special tree, a Brazilian Fig, in the Royal Botanical Gardens. A self-described tree hugger, he has been quoted as saying 'I like to ground myself and connect with that old friend' and 'I liked its roots and the trunk and branches and everything, so I started climbing it years ago. That's it. I have a connection.'[25] I am not suggesting that he wins tournaments and gains prowess and strength solely from being with a tree, but if we look at other famous humans in history who

24 Guiness World Records (2017). *Largest tree hug*. www.guinnessworldrecords.com/world-records/largest-tree-hug
25 Ben Church (2024). *Novak Djokovic: How a 'special relationship' with a tree is helping tennis star's bid for history at the Australian Open*. CNN Sports. edition.cnn.com/2024/01/19/sport/novak-djokovic-australian-open-tree-hugging-spt-intl

have benefitted from such association, it must be considered a great advantage. For instance, the great Buddha sought enlightenment while meditating beneath a fig tree and Isaac Newton formulated the law of gravitation while in the shade of an apple tree. Coincidence, perhaps, but I think not. Perhaps when Mr Djokovic retires from tennis, he will be the patron for an international tree huggers' association.

Tree houses

I predict there will be an explosion of demand for these and not the 4×4-foot child's cubby house style. Small house-size tree houses will be in demand for those who have the money and situations appropriate for their construction. I can see farmers supplementing their incomes with tree-mounted bed and breakfast accommodations. National parks and forest reserves are ideally placed to do the same. Visitors could customise their tree house stays by choosing those in trees that relate to them, making for a more rewarding experience. Health and wellness resorts will look to expand their appeal by liaising with tree house builders to build multiple tree house dwellings. I suggest these will be most attractive to the growing number of people who suffer from breathing conditions, especially if the trees in which the dwellings are built are related to *respiratrees*. Imagine the boom that will happen in tropical holiday destinations. From the Maldives in the Indian Ocean to the Whitsunday regions in Queensland and the islands of the Pacific Ocean and Hawaii, resorts will lure travellers with a free session with their resident *palmistree* guru, held in specialist tree houses built in palm trees. One can only imagine the frenzy this will cause in other Australian holiday destinations such as Bali, Thailand and regions of Asia. I am not qualified to give financial advice, but I feel confident in predicting it will not be long before tree house enterprises provide stock market investors with *treemendous* returns!

Building Design

Earlier in this work, the word biophilia was briefly mentioned. Biophilic architecture is now a well-defined field, and it will increase exponentially as its benefits become more widely known. Biophilic buildings are designed to create more productive and healthier environments and connect occupants more closely with nature by incorporating natural lighting, ventilation, landscape features and other elements. An example of the effects of biophilic architecture was shown in a 2014 case study of an administration office building at the University of Oregon USA, which reported a 10% reduction in office worker absenteeism. The influence of biophilic design will be seen in the buildings referred to in this chapter under the heading *Forestree*.

Landscapers

In the future, trees planted in domestic gardens will be treated with the respect of long-lost loved ones. A regular sight will be someone arriving home from work and immediately hugging their tree before acknowledging the eagerly awaiting dog, who has learned their place lower down the mammalian pecking order. Landscape designers will consider their client's *ancestree* and select species of tree that are in tune with their heritage, resulting in a feeling of familial harmony in the garden. For example, garden designers will select mainly deciduous trees for people whose tree DNA shows that they are primarily the descendants of deciduous trees. This process will take a lot of guesswork out of the tree selection process and will result in far fewer large trees being cut down because the garden owners just do not have an affinity for the species. I have heard of many people from the southern states of Australia selling up to move to Queensland, because they wanted to escape the southern winters for the northern warmth, only to return a few years later because they missed the distinctive changes of the seasons. This is no doubt the result of their deciduous *ancestree* exerting its powerful unseen force to return them to their roots.

The environment

As mentioned earlier, each year, around 15 billion trees are lost worldwide because of human actions. That is more than 41 million trees per day. The sad outcome of this is that the worldwide numbers of trees are estimated to be down to 52% of what they were only 2 centuries ago, when the world's human population was around one billion. The population of humans is now over 7 billion and rising rapidly. Again, it does not require great thought to understand that the vast majority of the people on the planet 200 years ago would have had little impact on their environments. In comparison, my guess would be that one average capitalist today – and I am one – would have at least ten times the negative impact on the environment than that of our forebears. So, from an environmental impact point of view, even if we estimate that there are only one billion capitalists in the world, we could say the effect of our current human population, living our current lifestyles, is up to 17 billion. This sobering thought leads to the other 'elephant in the room' - overpopulation. This subject is taboo in capitalist *countrees*, as population growth is fundamentally tied to economic growth. It has to be addressed.

Recycling

While attempts are being made to reduce the human impact on our planet by recycling waste, there is so much more that can and needs to be done. At a household level, there are some encouraging projects that aim to repurpose plastic bags and glass. For example, The Curby's soft plastic recycling program is an initiative of concerned residents from the central coast of New South Wales. Consumers collect their soft plastics bags and accumulate them in a special bag that, when full, is put into the general recycling bin that is collected by the local council. When the recycling vehicle unloads its contents at the recycling facility, these bags are isolated and then sent to the facilities that repurpose the plastic into new materials.

The transition to alternative power sources for road vehicles is advancing rapidly, with all major worldwide car manufacturers now producing hybrid and electric vehicles (EVs). The likely drop off in demand for fossil fuelled vehicles raises a potential problem, as one of the by-products of fuel production is tar, a key ingredient in making roads. A substitute will need to be found to create consistent road substrates. In Adelaide, a road in the suburb of Happy Valley has been constructed using 139,000 plastic bags, 39,000 plastic bottles, toner from approximately 3,200 used printer cartridges and 50 tonnes of recycled asphalt.[26] On a bigger scale, more than 797,000 recycled glass bottles

26 Downer (2018). *First South Australian Road built with soft plastics and glass.* https://www.downergroup. com/first-south-australian-road-built-with-soft-p

were used in a section of Adelaide's South Road rehabilitation works.[27] What better way to recycle waste than to divert it into something that will be needed and maintained for many years to come? There are many other examples of using recyclables in this way, giving hope that we are on a pathway to a more sustainable future.

In South Australia, from the Clare Valley and the Barossa in the north, to the Coonawarra, Langhorne Creek and McLaren Vale regions in the south, we are blessed with an abundance of wineries that produce world class produce. Most of the wineries in these regions have a rough, winding earthen road that leads to the cellar door. There must be some unwritten law as to why they do not have a nice, paved or sealed entranceway, possibly because of cost, but I suspect it has more to do with the rusticity of the experience. These wineries consume large quantities of glass bottles. I would like to plant the idea that at some point, some entrepreneurial winemaker will be the first to construct an all-weather entranceway with recycled glass, made using bottles of its own product range that have been returned. There are various ways they could go about accumulating the numbers they would need, such as offering a discount on additional purchases, or special bonus bottles based on each dozen bought. They could even set up a scheme like The Curby's recycling project mentioned above. I feel certain the effort will pay dividends when visitors read the history as to the road's construction and appreciate the environmental awareness and responsibility of the business involved. Not to mention that most visitors may appreciate arriving at the cellar door without being covered in dust during the summer months or having their car spattered with muddy water in the winters. It may take a while, but it wasn't long ago that the idea of selling wine in a bottle with a screwcap was laughed at by many.

At an individual level, we all need to take much more responsibility for the mess we make, and a good place to start is by understanding some basic fundamentals of recycling. For example, householders in South Australia can sort their waste into one of three different

27 AdelaideAZ. *Hundreds of thousands of recycled glass bottles incorporated into the asphalt for major South Australian roadworks.* adelaideaz.com/articles/hundreds-of-thousands-of-recycled-glass-bottles-incorporated-into-asphalt-for-major-south-australian-road-projects

waste bins, regularly collected from the kerbside by council-appointed contractors. One bin is for general rubbish, one for recyclable materials, and the third is for green waste and food scraps. The concept sounds simple, but unfortunately, so too are many people. Through ignorance or a complete lack of social responsibility, many people put the wrong things in the various bins. These mix-ups nullify the efforts of all those who do the right thing, because they taint the entire contents of the vehicle collecting potentially reusable waste, and it generally ends up going to landfill. Collectively, across the councils in Adelaide alone, poor bin behaviour costs councils an extra $20 million each year. In Adelaide alone, each year about 1.2 million tonnes of waste is generated each year, of which 35% is recycled. With a population of 1.3 million, this equates to each person dumping 1.2 kg of rubbish a day.[28] In 2018, as part of its National Sword Operation, China blocked the import of recyclable materials from many *countrees* in which contaminants constituted more than 0.5% of the waste. At the time, Australia was sending 619,000 tonnes of waste, worth $523 million to China annually.[29] Although not the only reason, the thoughtless actions of a minority at a household level no doubt contributed to this action. Perhaps some of the following suggestions may help to ensure recycling materials collected in the future consistently meet the criteria required for China to accept material from Australia again. Even allowing for behavioural tree vaccine therapies, my fear is it may take many years of human evolution to breed out the negative behaviours of many. It is very difficult to fix stupid!

Progress can still be made with recycling using a 'carrot and stick' approach as per the following scenario. Each residents' bins will be barcoded to link them with a specific address. Each time there is a waste pickup, the vehicle will scan and register the collection. As each council budgets for a certain number of collections per household, per year, a financial incentive via a rate reduction in the following year could be

28 Beau Schultz (2023). *An In-depth Look at Adelaide's Waste and Recycling Statistics.* Best Price Skip Bins. bestpriceskipbins.com.au/adelaide-waste-and-recycling-statistics/
29 Hopgood Ganim Lawyers (2018). *Impacts of China's 'Green Sword' Policy on Australia's Waste Disposal.* www.hopgoodganim.com.au/news-insights/impacts-of-chinas-green-sword-policy-on-australias-waste-disposal

applied, based on how many times a residence does not need their bin emptied. This is the 'carrot' part. Inevitably, there will be some who will do the wrong thing by dumping their rubbish elsewhere or making clandestine visits to dispose of their waste in a neighbour's bin the night before waste collection. So, the 'stick' part of the strategy will be larger fines for illegal dumping, with lesser but still significant fines for those who cheat on their neighbours. One way to mitigate this would be to have each bin fitted with a device that locks the lid, unlocks it when the rubbish truck scans it for collection, then closes and locks it after it has been emptied. There is a business opportunity here for security surveillance companies to make a fortune selling systems aimed at catching petty nocturnal bin invaders. The technology to implement such a scheme is already being used by the Horsham Rural City Council in Victoria.[30] Known as the RFID tag in your rubbish bin initiative, a small plastic device inserted under the lip of the bin contains a serial number specific to that bin. This tag allows waste collection trucks to identify whether the bin is at the correct property address, the time of collection and importantly, if the same bin has been presented multiple times on the same day. As education is an important factor for getting people to responsibly recycle, this needs to be a key component in the early years of our children's education.

Inside homes, waterless composting toilets will gradually replace the current flushing systems. Already in use throughout countries like Africa and India, waterless toilets play a significant role in reducing waterborne diseases and water wastage. These self-contained systems are compact, lightweight, hygienic, low maintenance and child safe. Importantly, they are environmentally friendly, as they do not need chemicals. A big plus is that they hygienically convert human waste into a suitable ingredient for fertilizer. Added to one's composting system, this is the ultimate form of recycling. Our oceans and marine life will be the main beneficiaries of the spread of this technology. Reductions in water and sewerage bills should encourage the uptake of this opportunity.

---

30 Horsham Rural City Council. *RFID Tags in Your Rubbish Bins.* https://www.hrcc.vic.gov.au/Our-Council/News-and-Media/Latest-News/RFID-tags-in-your-rubbish-bins

Solar power

This is one way we can continue to reduce the production of greenhouse gases, and in Australia, this technology has been widely supported. This has no doubt been accelerated, at least in Australia, by the financial lure of being paid for 'selling' excess power back into the grid. In the same way, in the future, householders may be able to receive a financial benefit based on the net oxygen output of trees planted on their property. To aid this process, in conjunction with biophilic architectural principles, new homes built in urban areas will be constructed with contained flat roofs to incorporate rooftop gardens. These will help to reduce each household's carbon footprint through oxygen created from the plants and reduced reliance on power for internal temperature control from the insulative capability of the roof plants and soil mass. Such practices will reduce the amount of heat our paved and concreted urban cities generate.

The therapeutic value of gardens of this type will go a long way in mitigating much of the stress, anxiety, addiction, isolation and general lack of direction experienced by so many in our cities. Rooftop gardening will become a new specialist field, incorporating structural design and construction components, soil, water collection and reticulation systems, garden design, plant selection, and seating areas to enjoy the views. Hydroponic gardening will be revitalised – with new satellite technologies employed to ensure that illegal propagation of banned plants does not occur! All households will be incentivised to install composting bins to provide natural fertiliser for their gardens and reduce the volume and collection cost of green waste. Where suitable, aesthetically designed rooftop wind generators, fitted with screens to prevent bird contact and accidental human injury, will boost power to batteries charged mainly by solar. Solar panel additions to existing metal or tiled roofs will continue, but we will soon see newly built homes with solar panels incorporated into a new product that replaces the need for current conventional roofing materials.

Motor vehicles will have solar panels incorporated into the roof and bonnet to augment battery power. This is not futuristic thinking. Companies such as Tesla have been testing various options for incorporating solar charging in their range of EVs. Apart from the additional cost saving for charging EVs, the benefits lie in either extending the current range limits or reducing the size and weight of current batteries, which will also help extend the range. As an indication of what is possible, in 1997, the inaugural World Solar Challenge for road vehicles utilising only solar power was held in Australia. Over 4–7 days these vehicles travelled the 3022 km from Darwin to Adelaide. Initially held every three years, it is now a biannual event. In 1996, team Honda won the event with an average speed of 88.5 km/h, and in 2005, the Dutch Nuna team became the first to break the 100km/h barrier, covering the distance at an average speed of 102.75 km/h.[31]

Similarly, passenger aircraft are ideally suited to have the upper fuselage and wing area act as solar power cells to reduce the amount of conventional jet fuel required once the aircraft reaches cruising altitudes. While this is not yet seen as viable for commercial aircraft, the fact that solar-powered aircraft are already in operation in research and surveillance activities suggests it won't be long before the technology is utilised in larger commercial aircraft. With up to an 80% reduction of fuel emissions currently achievable and the drive to cut down fossil fuel usage to curb global warning, I predict we will soon see aircraft fuselages made from materials housing solar receptors.

First Australians

First Australians have lived in this nation for at least 60,000 years. After all that time, their imprint on the land has been almost undetectable. By comparison, in a little over 200 years, white settlement has initiated changes to our environment that, if continued unabated, will eventually render much of our *countree* uninhabitable. The learnings of our oldest culture must be respected, preserved, understood, and taught if we are to have a genuine appreciation and respect for our land and its unique flora and fauna. From the chapter 'Thoughts for My Son' in the illuminating book Phosphorescence, Australian author Julia Baird sums this up beautifully:

---

31 Wikipedia. *Nuna 3*. https://en.wikipedia.org/wiki/Nuna_3

... he should respect the 60,000-year history of this country, listen to the lament of its original inhabitants, recognise their rightful, central place in our land, and lean against those who would block, mute, resist or diminish them.[32]

Throughout my school years in Adelaide, we were taught the *histree* of bygone civilizations from Egypt, Greece, the Romans and doubtless others that I fail to remember, but not one word about our first inhabitants. Thankfully, this has changed. As recently as 2024, Australia's largest state (New South Wales) has now made education about aboriginal cultures and histories *mandatree* in every compulsory year of education (kindergarten to year 10).

These curriculum reforms herald a commitment by educators to tell the full story of our past. All students will benefit from a thorough knowledge and appreciation of this ancient land, the depth and beauty of our Aboriginal past, the truth about the harsh colonial dispossession of the original owners and of the rich Aboriginal cultures and communities that still endure.[33]

On a broader note, Amnesty International reports that there are around 476 million indigenous people around the world, incorporating over 5,000 different cultural and ethnic groups and more than 4,000 different languages from 90 *countrees*. The experience and wisdom of all indigenous peoples across the globe must be recorded, understood and taught in their *countrees'* schools, with practical outcomes from the lessons learned being actioned.

I hope that awareness of the history of Australia's First Peoples, irrespective of whether their ancestral links are tied to koalas or not, results in an influx of overseas visitors coming to Australia to learn firsthand about their culture, beliefs and history.

---

32 Julia Baird (2020, p. 206–207). *Phosphorescence: On Awe, Wonder and Things That Sustain You When the World Goes Dark.* HarperCollins.

33 Education International (2024). *Australia: Aboriginal Cultures and Histories now Central to Education.* https://www.ei-ie.org/en/item/29006:australia-aboriginal-cultures-and-histories-now-central-to-education

I have deliberately chosen this section to be the last on the long list of topics in this chapter because it is more likely to be remembered that way. The whole concept of this work is based on new theories as to human evolution, and the 60,000-year plus lineage of the First Australians may just be the key factor in unravelling and redefining human *histree*.

❧❧❧

THE THEORY OF TREEVOLUTION POTENTIAL ADVERSE CONSEQUENCES

∼∽∕∖∾∾

I t would be appropriate for me to mention some of the potential adverse consequences that may arise from the uptake of the ideas and suggestions put forward in this theory.

As with any new medical, scientific and technological progress, there are inherent dangers, mostly caused through flaws in human nature. Sometimes, great ideas and advances in the areas of human progress throw out undesirable consequences that are difficult to predict and once they take hold, are difficult to correct. For all its positives and benefits, the internet has its undesirable aspects – leaking of personal data to scammers, online bullying, predators lurking to trap people in their webs of debauchery, dubious dating sites, fraudulent advertising and scams to defraud people of their money, just to list a few.

Cosmetic surgery

With the advances in medicine of cosmetic surgery, we have all seen images of people who have undergone surgery to alter some perceived body imperfection. These procedures are often undertaken in a futile attempt to make people feel better about themselves and sometimes result in regret. I have often wondered if I'm the only one who thinks people who have lip fillers in their lips (which makes many of them look as though they have just had a bad reaction to kissing the wrong end of a highly aggravated European wasp), ostensibly to look more attractive to the opposite sex, end up achieving the reverse? Apart from sounding slightly intoxicated when they speak, to add insult to injury, many also have Botox injected into their forehead, the end result being that when they speak, they often look and sound like a drunken ventriloquist's dummy! Just so I am not condemned for being sexist by inferring that only woman have cosmetic procedures that go awry, many of the above comments could be deemed to include the late Michael Jackson (except the bit about the wasp).

As for science, I dread to think what warped outcomes we could see once unscrupulous scientists start tinkering with different tree DNA in humans. Hopefully, by the time someone transcribes this book into other languages, the Western world will be well advanced in the ethical use of this work. Besides, I am hopeful non-Western rulers would think much of what I have written is in code and I wish them well trying to decipher the meaning of some of my diatribes.

Genetic engineering

Many years ago, an expression often used in response to someone saying something startling or unexpected was 'are you for real'? For the uninitiated, the expression meant 'are you kidding me'? I have the distinct feeling that this expression will come back into regular usage in the near future with a very different meaning. This time it will mean what it states. With so many people now having operations from cosmetic surgery to hip and knee replacements, insertions of cardiac stents and pacemakers and major organ transplants, I can see the time when a young person trying to chat up a prospective mate will be thinking, if not asking, if they are for real. The genetic altering of a person's character through the medical application of tree-DNA-changing medication may add just another layer of complexity. One could be forgiven for wondering whether the person of their interest or desire is behaving naturally or if they are a recently released psychotic nut case whose inner character has been temporarily suppressed with balancing tree elixirs.

Hair styling

The industries that have evolved around supplying hair products, cutting and styling services and the money that is spent worldwide is surely out of proportion to any actual benefit for our wellbeing or survival as a species. Again, this an example of just how powerful our ancestral roots can be. Our often-desperate desire to return our forest crown to its youth paves the way for unscrupulous enterprises to make fortunes with potions and procedures promising to restore the former glory of your balding pate. With regard to the opportunities mentioned earlier to effectively cure baldness, there must be carefully considered government safeguards, laws and protocols to ensure a plethora of bogus enterprises with outlandish claims and false ingredients do not overtake the market. This currently happens in Australia with health food supplements. Some years ago, the Australian Therapeutics Goods Act was established to prevent such instances occurring. All therapeutic goods manufactured and sold in Australia must be either registered or listed (awarded an Aust R or Aust L number, respectively), depending on the nature of the advertising claims and efficacy of the product based on medical and scientific studies. However, they are powerless to stop the flood of vitamin preparations flooding in from overseas destinations via the internet, which are often accompanied with outlandish claims. My advice to anyone who receives mail from a source that claims their product is scientifically proven to cure just about everything under the sun, supported by happy smiling faces and glowing endorsements from bogus customers, is to dispose of the literature in the recycle bin or return to sender with a note to stick their promises where the sun doesn't shine, or at least a thank you note for supporting the Australian postal system.

Real estate sales

The downside to planting one of your distant tree relatives in your own garden may be an emotional impact evoked if and when you have to sell the home and move on. If one is very attached to their tree, imagine the guilt if one day you drove past your former home to find that your loved one has been hewn down and replaced by another species. On the other hand, a potential buyer may be looking for a home with an established tree that has the characteristics of the one you have, which would be a win-win for both parties.

In the future, I can see clauses added to contracts of sale, and even wills, covering these issues.

Tree houses

Site and tree suitability will be at a premium once the tree-house revolution takes hold. I suspect that to meet demand and/or avoid costs, some entrepreneurs will install what I call quasi tree houses. These would look like tree houses and be raised up amongst the trees, but they will be attached to pylons or timber posts and not the actual trees. Still, if such residences can offer an enhanced view and the experience feels like a tree house, I do not see too great a downside. If the *forestree* ideas mentioned previously are implemented, there will eventually be plenty of areas to setup tree houses once the forests become established.

Law and order

With the reduction in crime rates, the drop off in divorce rates and the decrease in people's stress levels in general leading to fewer civil actions, there will be less work for the legal fraternity. However, I am sure it would not take long for some enterprising legal firms to find an opportunity to help felons escape criminal charges by arguing that their tree *ancestree* is to blame for their actions. Hopefully, any underemployed lawyers and judges will substitute lawsuits and trials for tree hugging in the park and running fundraisers for their local council tree house projects – in between addressing the occasional situation that requires their expertise, of course. With new *treetments* available to break addiction habits, casinos, hotels and community clubs will gradually begin to lose some patronage and income. This will come about as people begin to realise that feeding their hard-earned money into insatiable metal black holes is not as much fun as wandering through forests in the fresh air, searching for rare species of flora and birds. Unfortunately, there will inevitably be some who will be disadvantaged for the greater good, but as a wise chef once said, 'you can't have omelettes for breakfast without cracking a few eggs.'

LIMITS OF TREEVOLUTION

❧❦❧

T he scope for positive change in people's lives outlined in previous chapters should give great optimism for the advancement of human civilization. However, some areas of the human condition may prove highly resistant to any behavioural treatments arising from treevolution. For example, if a survey was put to a large group of married women with the question 'if you could change two things in your male partner that would alleviate stress from your life, what would they be'? I am sure the following two responses would be at, or near, the top of the list.

- The first would be to overcome their partner's consistent inability to recall the location of their wallet, phone, car keys, sunglasses, watch, reading glasses, etc., just as they are about to go out the front door. The propensity for this to occur increases in direct proportion to the urgency of the departure deadline. Frustrating though this must be, as a man afflicted with this condition, I can assure women that we do not enjoy the humiliation ensuing from this situation, and it is not done deliberately.

- The second would be to have their partner utilise his opposable thumbs to change the toilet roll and dispose of the spent cardboard cylinder appropriately. On this point, I do have some credibility; I wrote a book on the issue some years ago, *Yes Men, You Can Change the Toilet Roll*.

The reason for the first situation lies in the differences in the way men's and women's brains have been configured over thousands of years of evolution to deal with basic survival. Only over the last century have men had to remember to collect these new necessities when they go out the front door. Up until then, all they needed was a gun and some ammunition, a bow and a few arrows, or a spear. Sadly, we have not evolved mentally (nor I suspect, emotionally) to keep up with modern technological demands and advancements. Women's brains, on the other hand, have evolved to be multi-dimensional – they remember everything. I once heard a man's apt definition of a wife as 'someone who can find a pair of socks that isn't there'. Before I am chastised for using this as a cop-out or being sexist, I would refer anyone interested in this topic to read an excellent book titled, *Why Men Don't Listen and Women Can't Read Roadmaps*, by Australian authors Allan and Barbara Pease. Implementing strategies learned from this and other sources will be a far better option for improving relationships than waiting several thousand years for evolution to catch up.

OBSERVATIONS AND CONCLUSIONS

❦❦❦

The many communication channels we have at our fingertips today constantly expose us to the devastating impacts of natural disasters. Forest fires, floods, landslides, tsunamis, volcanic eruptions and cyclones constantly remind us of nature's destructive power. Nature also displays its power in ways that are much less noticeable and dramatic, since they occur over longer periods of time. For instance, water erosion creating spectacular ravines and canyons, and the force of glacial ice, strong enough to carve out valleys. One of the greatest examples of nature's power I have ever experienced was many years ago during a school science lesson, when I held a few tree seeds in the palm of my hand. They were so small and light that I could barely feel their weight, yet I knew they could grow into giants that might live for hundreds of years. Once sprouted, they would start their life's work of storing carbon, cleansing the air, bringing joy to those fortunate enough to see and appreciate them, and doing their level best to ensure their species continued to thrive. My mind is too primitive to even begin to contemplate the unique blueprint and the powerful forces that lie within such tiny seeds. It might seem surprising, but I really have no real desire to ever understand the how and why. Just knowing is enough.

However, I would love to see some of the world's great trees if the opportunity ever arises. One day, I might visit the world's tallest living tree, a giant coast redwood in Northern California. The tree, named 'Hyperion' has grown to a height of 115.7 metres from a seed only 3 mm long. Then there is 'General Sherman', a giant sequoia located in the Giant Forest of Sequoia National Park in California, which grew from a seed less than 5 mm long. Now 2,000 years old, it is 83.8 metres tall with a girth at chest height of 24.1 metres, making it the world's largest living tree.

If such tiny seeds have this incredible force within them, what else could they be capable of? Why couldn't the forest trees that spring from this power have the means to communicate with us on some telepathic or other subconscious level, in ways we have yet to understand? Could they possess the knowledge, wisdom and power to have influenced humans like Jesus, Buddha and Newton? If they could do this, then they certainly could have influenced the English to unknowingly develop their language so it contained a clear link between humans and trees. It is probable this all stemmed from times just prior to the industrial revolution, when the wise trees of the forests could see that their human descendants were embarking on a dangerous path that could lead to their eventual demise, and ultimately to the destruction of many of the Earth's plants, trees and creatures as well. Could they have colluded to leave these links in the English language as a message and a warning, hoping someone would make the connection to the importance of recognising and not forsaking our origins? Is it their plan to jolt us back to a way of living more sustainably by being attuned to and living in balance with nature?

A clear answer to this question was revealed to me well over a year after I wrote the manuscript containing the above question. I sent out my 'seeds' of treevolution, hoping to find fertile ground (a publisher) willing to take on my work. After enduring the silence of rejection that all writers aspiring to make their voice heard must face, I became disheartened and moved on with other areas of my life to help fill the void of frustration, disappointment and failure. Still, for some reason, without me being aware of it, treevolution began to creep back into my mind, like a gentle but persistent tap on the shoulder to get my attention. The strength of this tap grew when I was drawn to read the book *Big Magic* by Elizabeth Gilbert of *Eat, Pray, Love* fame. After reading her story, I had the necessary 'kick up the bum' to revisit my work anew. Not long after, I came across the remarkable work of Monica Gagliano, PhD, an Australian research scientist with academic credentials as long as your proverbial arm. Her book, *Thus Spoke the Plant*, gave me a whole new perspective on trees and plants, a sense of validation in what I was writing, and the emotional fuel to bring treevolution to life. Here was a highly qualified woman who communicated with the vegetal world. A woman with a spiritual connection to trees and plants that 'talked' to her, not through audible sounds, but with some kind of telepathic mind transfer, guiding her quest to find scientific answers. She showed that plants and trees have the same senses of hearing, sight, smell and touch, and the ability to learn, remember and adapt to environmental changes as any other living creature, including, and especially – us. One particular Socoba tree (*Himatanthus sucuuba*), a tropical tree revered by the Shipibo people of Peru, revealed to her that it 'was a blood cleanser, the healer of conditions that affected the blood and the network of vessels that assure the smooth flowing of blood inside the human body.'[34] Could it just be that this species is related to or are *circulatrees* or *artrees*? I have never met or spoken to Dr Gagliano, nor am I attempting to compare my theory based on my thoughts and other readily available information to her body of discoveries based on the outcomes of professional research conducted according to appropriate protocols. I would gladly take the chance to meet her some day for a chat, even at the risk of discovering that she felt I should be sent to a sanitorium for counselling with a *psychiatree*!

With the exception of gravity, the only comparison to the quiet and sustained power of trees that I have observed in all my years on this planet is the power of love that women have for their family, particularly their children. Throughout my own marriage and now with my daughter, I have observed the patience, vigilance, absolute devotion, intuitive wisdom, ability to survive mind-numbing tedium and self-sacrifice needed to raise the next generation. I can now see the correlation with our tree ancestors that only furthers my conviction that we are their descendants. It's not that men generally do not have these traits as well. It's just that, overall, we do not have the requisite levels of patience, concentration, endurance, vigilance and consistency as women when it comes to our offspring. If the survival of humanity depended on men like me – who have the memory span of a goldfish and attentive ability of a Sidchrome spanner (I have taken the liberty

34 Monica Gagliano (2018, p. 12). *Thus Spoke The Plant: A Remarkable Journey of Groundbreaking Scientific Discoveries and Personal Encounters with Plants*. North Atlantic Books.

here of according myself a reputable brand) – the human species would in all probability die out in a relatively short period of time. I have come to the conclusion that if the Christian concept of a loving God truly exists, then that God must surely be female. In this regard, despite my previous rantings about the growing demascularisation of the English language, I would be in favour of changing every word in the Bible relating to God from He/Him to She/Her and ending every church prayer with 'A-Woman'.

Irrespective of your thoughts about the validity or otherwise of the theory of treevolution, I hope that, if nothing else, we will look at trees with a new-found respect. We need to understand that trees can live without humans, but we cannot survive without them. It may come as a surprise to many, that there would not be enough oxygen in the atmosphere to support human life if not for the process of photosynthesis that has been quietly occurring within the world's plants and trees over millions of years. Creatures like us would never have been able to evolve and survive without them. Irrespective of what we believe our origins to be, all humans share a crucial link in everyday living with trees. We need to breathe in oxygen and exhale carbon dioxide, whereas trees absorb carbon dioxide and release oxygen back into the air.

Humans and trees are co-dependent – we effectively breathe each other in and out, one surviving on the exhalation of the other.

While debates about climate change and carbon quotas rage on, with an estimated decline each year of over ten billion trees worldwide, we are paying a high price for effectively destroying the lungs of our planet. It is no coincidence that today, Chronic Obstructive Pulmonary Disease (COPD) is the fourth leading cause of death and disease burden in humans. Currently affecting 1 in 7 Australians over the age of 40, this incurable disease is the second leading cause of avoidable hospital admissions. With millions of trees being cut down daily, it becomes blatantly obvious why we are seeing rising surface temperatures, rising sea levels caused by the melting of the polar ice caps and alarming rises in levels of carbon dioxide and other far more noxious man-made gases in the atmosphere.

I hope that one of the key facilitators of the economic growth killing our planet may yet hold the key to its survival. It has largely been through access to the internet that I have been able to resource and read the material, confirm facts and pull together the information needed to produce this work. Importantly, it has allowed me to see there are millions of like-minded people wrestling with the same concerns and feelings I am experiencing. Through this medium, I hope these people can unite and bring pressure to bear, in a peaceful way, on our leaders to see the dire inevitability of our current political and economic systems and cooperatively work to balance economic pressures and capitalist expectations with the needs of our environment. Sacrifices will have to be made. As consumers, we will all need to come to terms with having less 'stuff'. However, once we all become more in-tune with our tree ancestors, I believe the need for materialism will begin to fade to a point where we all become much happier human 'treeings'.

EPILOGUE

When I wrote the section on Histree in the chapter Treevolution and the Future, it becomes apparent that my thoughts on the origins and meanings of the word had changed dramatically from what I wrote in the earlier part of this book. Many may consider my words then to be the rantings of a misogynistic, chauvinistic pig. And so, the obvious question arises: why didn't I delete it from the manuscript? The answer to this question holds the key to one of the major purposes of writing this work. I left it in to show that we can and must change our attitudes and actions towards many current world issues. I once noticed a message chalked on one of those A-frame boards outside a shop some years ago, that struck me: *When you change the way you look at things, the things you look at change.* We humans need to question our thinking on so many aspects of our lives in order to change, if for no other reason than to leave a planet on which future generations can live.

In the Introduction to this book, I mentioned there was another reason why I decided to write the theory of treevolution. As one gets older and the pressures of day to day living ease, our thoughts turn to other important life issues. One of those is the inevitability of our time running out. We are thus led, either gently, or forcibly, to look at how we might choose to be *treeted* when we pass on from this world. My wish is to be buried under a tree, possibly of the species from which I descended, so that my grandchildren can occasionally visit 'Granddad' and give him a big hug, while still seeing him as a vibrant living entity. To know that in 20, 50 or 100 years or more I *wood* have contributed nutrients to the life of a tree that still brings beauty to the world as it continues trapping carbon in its body while cleaning the air around it - now that *wood* be a wondrous legacy. At present, there is no legal facility for this to happen in Australia, so I would like to start a foundation for this to be available. Somehow, I hope the writing of this work could be the catalyst that helps make this an option for others of like mind, through the creation of the first Tree *Cemetree*, hopefully somewhere in the beautiful Adelaide Hills.

I also stated I had no understanding of how or why this idea picked me instead of any one of millions of other, more capable people. Pure chance most likely, the *lottree* of life, just as a seed in the wind has no control over where it will land and must deal with what fate hands it in its drive for survival. In that sense, this work is just like a tree seed. It will land somewhere, someone will read it, and in all probability, it will then be stuffed in a cupboard or on a shelf, and that will be the end of its ability to take root and potentially make a positive contribution to humanity. Hopefully, enough of these seeds will fall into the hands of people who have the fertile minds and the means to bring about the changes we need to bring human behaviour back into balance with nature. This will enable our future generations to look forward to a pollution free, oxygenated and tree-filled life on this wonderful planet.

In my introduction, I also stated that one of the reasons for not commencing this project many years earlier was timing. In this regard, as I draw near completion of this work in May 2025, I believe the right time to put the messages of our true ancestors out into the world is now. In the space of just a few years, the human world has changed. The coronavirus pandemic exposed the fragility of human life and many of the structures we rely on to support it. The *monetree* systems that bind our *countrees* are teetering on collapse, putting the livelihoods of millions of people at risk. The financial world is entering an unchartered period of deflation or negative growth. Governments are trying to stop the haemorrhaging of their economies by bolstering businesses and livelihoods with money borrowed from future generations. In the aftermath of the corona virus pandemic, businesses have returned to some semblance of normal and in many ways, life may appear for most to have returned to what it was a few short years ago. However, I cannot help but feel we are in the relative but false calm of the so-called 'eye of the storm'. Now is the time for our international leaders to reset objectives and systems by incorporating the wisdom of indigenous peoples and our tree ancestors. The primary guiding principles must always be centred on ensuring that Mother Nature comes first.

I hope governments will be proactive in initiating, funding and supporting the private sector in many of the initiatives I have suggested. Many displaced people will find new lives, happiness and a sense of purpose in being part of:

- *forestree* careers
- the tree house industry
- bringing peace to the middle east with new infrastructure and sport
- restructuring school and university curriculums to embrace nature, the environment and the wisdom of our true ancestors
- training people to appreciate the practices of tree-hugging and forest bathing
- managing the growth of tree *cemetrees*, which will be linked to the acceptance and growth of euthanasia, and
- prolonging the need for this last option by refocusing our medical professionals to study the wisdom of the natural world to improve our health and wellbeing.

As I near the end of the theory of treevolution, it would be prudent to respond to one question that anyone who has read this far could be expected to have in mind. Does this guy really believe humans are descended from trees, or is he just some nutter trying to mess with our heads?

There are very few things in life I can say with full conviction that I believe unconditionally. The obvious ones are death and taxes, along with the hard-earned knowledge (eventually gained during my youth) that gravity never ever, even for a millisecond, takes time off. In the chapter The Rise of Mammals, I expressed the notion that with my surname and European origins, I may have descended from deer, but an incident a few years ago dashed any hope of this. I was holding one of my young grandsons on a trip to the city one day, when I almost toppled over as I lost my footing when I crossed some tram tracks (legally of course). I heard a snap in my left lower leg and felt like I had just been shot. Fast forward a trip to the doctor, who informed me that I had snapped the monkey muscle in my left calf. I thought he was joking, until he explained what it was – an outdated piece of sinew designed to provide lateral stability to our legs when our distant ancestors were climbing trees! On reflection, at that time, my disappointment at the realisation of not being related to one of Santa's reindeer was tempered with the knowledge that at least this confirmed I must have come from a line of primates that probably evolved in Europe – from European trees. Oddly enough, it wasn't until I was writing these words that distant and long-buried memories came to mind of the wonderful times I had climbing trees in my youth. I had many stayovers at my grandparents' home, which was bounded on three sides by the Kooyonga golf course in the Adelaide suburb of Lockleys. My older brother and I often hopped the fence to climb the tall pine trees, daring each other to climb higher between scurrying back down to dart across the fairway to snatch a golf ball plonked temptingly close to us by some poor unsuspecting golfer. While at home we climbed the one tree in our front garden that was tall enough to enable access to the tiled roof. Then, on warm summer Sundays, we joined other kids in the Belair National Park to go wild, climbing all of those beautiful European trees planted by the early pioneers. With all those recollections, I can now see my primate connection and realise just how fortunate I was to have had the freedom to enjoy those experiences seldom experienced by most of today's youth.

The rapidly disappearing monkey muscle, along with the palmaris longus (wrist muscle used by our ancestors to provide stability in tree climbing) and coccyx (along with recorded events of humans being born with a vestigial tail) are ancient links to our tree ancestors and subtle reminders for the imbued forces within humans that bind us in our love for trees. Still, the question remains as to where and from what did our primate ancestors evolve? Perhaps that small shrew mammal that looks at this stage to be the likely ancestor of primates came from a smaller creature again that evolved from trees. I cannot say categorically that I believe we all came from trees, but I can believe in the possibility that this may someday be proven correct. In the meantime, I can at least live with some degree of contentment in the knowledge that if I do not have a direct tree lineage, I am at least born of trees.

Our planet was formed about 4.5 billion years ago. The first signs of life can be traced back to around 3.7 billion years. For most people, including me, it would be a fair guess to say our brains cannot comprehend the magnitude of such numbers, let alone the powerful cosmic forces that enabled our world to form and life to evolve. All life forms on this earth are subject to laws and influences from these same cosmic forces, some that we think we understand and many I suspect we do not. If we humans are to remain as a viable species into the future, we need to come to terms with these laws and understand that we need to live in unison with them, instead of trying to manipulate, ignore or control them. Mankind's natural drive to explore the universe searching for knowledge and seeking answers to some of life's most perplexing questions may not need to extend to the planets and stars in outer space. The answers to questions such as, where did we come from, is there a God, are there other intelligent life forms out there in the cosmos and is there life after death, may be answered by communicating with trees here on Earth. What wisdom and knowledge could be gleaned from trees whose species originated millions of years ago? Could Ginkgo trees (270 million years), Wollemi pines (200 million years), Bunya pines (100 million years), Dawn Redwoods (57 million years) and many others, be *planetrees* or *interplanetrees* and hold the answers to these questions? Is it possible they have the knowledge we seek because they themselves originated on other worlds before travelling through space and time to give life to our planet? Where better to look for knowledge, wisdom and guidance than abundant sources that trace back millions of years and yet are right under our proverbial noses?

It has been said one of the greatest legacies one can leave is to plant a tree, knowing that you will never live to walk under its shade.[35] With this in mind, I hope some of the ideas raised in this book will be well

---

35 Attributed to a Canadian farmer, Nelson Henderson, who said, 'The true meaning of life is to plant trees under whose shade you do not expect to sit'. I think it likely he paraphrased the words of an Indian poet, Rabindranath Tagore, who wrote, 'The one who plants trees, knowing that he will never sit in their shade, has at least started to understand the meaning of life'.

on the way to becoming a reality by the time I fall off the proverbial perch. I also hope that many more will take root and keep evolving long after I have vacated this magnificent world. Perhaps one day in the not-too-distant future, I will be drawn to the television – hopefully distracting me from my efforts to hot-up my mobility scooter before the annual Shady Acres Retirement Home gopher race – to see and hear that one of my ideas has, or is, growing to fruition. That would be all I could ever ask for. Who knows, even then, it may still be possible to buy a mango! There is always hope.

It is worth repeating the wise saying, 'when you change the way you look at things, the things you look at change'. It is time for us to look at trees from a different mindset. It is time for the wisdom of the Great Trees of our world to be heard and understood, and the lessons learned put into action – before it is too late.

If you have learned a few interesting things you did not know, or more importantly, gained a greater understanding and appreciation for trees, then the writing of this theory will have been worthwhile. With reverence for trees the world over, I could not think of a more appropriate conclusion than to cite these words from an old song, *Wooden Heart*[36]:

---

36 Written and first sung by an American, Joe Dowel and later sung by Elvis Presley.

＊＊／＼＊＊

Treet me nice

Treet me good

Treet me like you really should

For though I'm made of *wood*[37]

I don't have a *wooden* Heart.

＊＊／＼＊＊

---

37 For the purists: I know, I've slightly altered the fourth line.

ACKNOWLEDGEMENTS

This book would never have come to light if not for the input of the following people:

Katie Lowe – Structural Editing and layout guidance

Lisa Chant – Editing and content advice

Matt Pike – my guide and mentor through the publication maze and for Cover and Back page design and production

Craig James from Black Canvas photographers – not just for the photo but also the countless times he helped with my many computer issues.

Last, but not least, **Deb Stagg** – my lifelong partner, my inspiration, my most honest critic and the most wonderful human treeing I have ever known.

BIBLIOGRAPHY

Much of the information for this work has come from readily available and what I deemed, credible sources found on the wonderful world of Google. As my writing is classified as 'Literary Fiction', I see no point in providing reference sources for every word, statement or claim in an attempt to make treevolution sound more credible or plausible. However, the following books may be of interest for anyone who wants to delve deeper into various aspects where they have been mentioned in the relevant chapters.

The Hidden Life of Trees	**Peter Wohlleben**
The Secret Life of Trees: How They Live and Why They Matter	**Colin Tudge**
Finding the Mother Tree: Discovering the Wisdom of the Forest	**Suzanne Simard**
Thus Spoke The Plant: A Remarkable Journey of Groundbreaking Scientific Discoveries and Personal Encounters with Plants	**Monica Gagliano**
The Bird Way: A New Look at how Birds Talk, Work, Play, Parent, and Think	**Jennifer Ackerman**
God Is Not Great	**Christopher Hitchens**
How to Fix The Future: Staying Human in the Digital Age	**Andrew Keen**
The Story of Trees	**Kevin Hobbs & David West**
Phosphorescence	**Julia Baird**
Blinded by Science	**Matthew Silverstone**
Why Men Don't Listen and Women Can't Read Roadmaps	**Allan and Barbara Pease**
The Edge of Memory: Ancient Stories, Oral Tradition and the Post-Glacial World	**Patrick Nunn**
Big Magic: How to Live a Creative Life, and Let Go of Your Fear	**Elizabeth Gilbert**

ABOUT THE AUTHOR

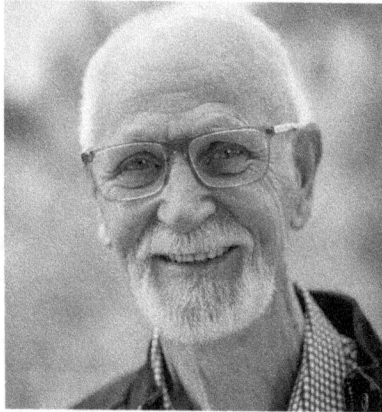

Christopher Stagg is 75 years young, having left the rigours of employment in sales and marketing at age 67. Retirement enabled him to focus on a long-held dream to be a published author of a work that is not just interesting and thought provoking, but also beneficial to humanity. Treevolution is the manifestation of this dream.

In 2003, he self-published a short work titled *Yes Men - You Can Change the Toilet Roll* (ISBN 0-9751657-0-4). Further, in 2007, he self-published his father's war memoirs of his time as a spitfire pilot embroiled in the defence of Darwin during the Second World War. (Titled *Caterpillar Club Survivor: Lost in the Top End, 1943* (ISBN 978-0-646-47777-0).

Other than writing, he enjoys visiting new places with his life partner, the interactions with his family, E-bike riding, volunteer work in the Belair National Park not far from his home near the Adelaide suburb of Blackwood and catching up for chats and coffee with old friends.

www.ingramcontent.com/pod-product-compliance
Lightning Source LLC
Chambersburg PA
CBHW032133020426
42334CB00016B/1153